THE CRUSADE OF

FÁTIMA

The Lady More Brilliant Than the Sun

*

BY

REV. JOHN DE MARCHI

Consolata Institute for Foreign Missions

*

ARRANGED FROM THE PORTUGUESE BY

REV. ASDRUBAL CASTELLO BRANCO

AND

REV. PHILIP C. M. KELLY, C.S.C.

1826

P. J. KENEDY & SONS · *NEW YORK*

Nihil Obstat:

    FRANCIS J. MALONEY, S.T.L., *Censor Librorum*

Imprimatur:

    ✠JAMES E. CASSIDY, *Bishop of Fall River*

August 11, 1947
Fall River, Mass.

DECLARATION

In conformity with the decree of Pope Urban VIII, we do not wish to anticipate the judgment of the Church in our appraisal of the characters and occurrences spoken of herein. We submit wholeheartedly to the infallible wisdom and judgment of Holy Mother Church.

———

Second Printing

TO THE

IMMACULATE HEART OF MARY

WHO APPEARED OVER THE HILLS OF AIRE

THE GREAT SIGN OF HEAVEN

A WOMAN CLOTHED WITH THE SUN

BRINGING TO THE WORLD

A NEW ERA OF

MERCY, PEACE AND LOVE

What has happened in Portugal, proclaims the miracle. It is the presage of what the Immaculate Heart has prepared for the world.

His Eminence, THE CARDINAL PATRIARCH OF LISBON

THE CRUSADE OF FÁTIMA

Statue of Our Lady
Shrine of Our Lady of Fátima
Cova da Iria, Portugal

Preface to the American Edition

EVERY NOW AND THEN in the course of history,
Almighty God has seen fit to intervene in some
marvellous way to shake mankind, so it seems, out
of his self-sufficiency into the realization of His
ever-present Sovereignty. These continual manifestations of God's Mercy help to keep alive in men's
hearts the reality of the spiritual.

All are familiar with the instance of Lourdes, with
its compelling message of faith and mercy to an age
of men who, in their intellectual pride, sought to
eliminate God and His Church from the affairs of
this world. More recently, and as if to anticipate our
present concern over the downward course of civili-
zation, God has again deigned to send His Blessed
Mother. This time she comes, not so much the
merciful healer as at Lourdes though she is always
that, but rather as the valiant protectress of all
things sacred. In these sad days of the twentieth
century, memorable for their widespread miseries
and merciless tyrannies, God would have mankind
look upward to the Heart of His Sorrowful Mother.
Only Our Blessed Mother, and not politicians or
armies, can give rest and peace to the hearts of men
and to the world which yearns for it so very much.

In 1917, during World War I, the Communistic
Revolution in Russia heralded the beginning of its
world-wide Anti-God crusade. At this same time,
Our Lady appeared to three little children as they

grazed their sheep along the barren hills of Fatima, Portugal. She came to start a counter-revolution— a crusade for God—and she called the world to penance and reparation, to prevent a future and worse world-conflict within the next generation. These little children were to lead the way to peace, in Mary's Immaculate Heart.

The account of these apparitions which follows consists mainly of the direct testimony of Lucia de Santos, the oldest of the three children to whom Our Lady appeared and manifested her thorn-pierced Heart. She is still living and is a member of the Sisters of St. Dorothy. She has written an accurate account of all happenings in her "Memoirs" at the direct command of her superiors. We include herein also the testimony of those other persons—parents, priests and witnesses—who in some way were involved in the apparitions or the lives of the children.

Foreword

THIS BOOK began as a translation of Father John De Marchi's long and authoritative account of the Fátima apparitions, *Era Uma Senhora Mais Brilhante Que O Sol*. The author of this book resides at the Shrine of Our Lady of Fátima and is a leader in the Crusade for Mary. He has spoken with every living witness of the apparitions, and has spent many hours conversing with two of the principal bystanders, Ti Marto, father of Francisco and Jacinta, and Maria da Capelinha, one of Fátima's earliest crusaders. Moreover, Father De Marchi's account has the unqualified endorsement of Lúcia de Jesús (now Sister Maria das Dores).

It became evident, however, as the work progressed, that some changes in the original account would be called for, if this book were to reach the wide public it deserved. First after having reviewed all available documents on Fátima, we gathered information which helped to throw new light on many passages and to bring out the full meaning and essential purpose of these apparitions:—the establishment throughout the world of the devotion to the Immaculate Heart of Mary and the personal consecration of every living soul to her loving service. It is true that the full account of Fátima would require many large volumes but then only the learned and erudite would read this beautiful message from Heaven. Therefore we desired that THE

ix

CRUSADE OF FATIMA be published in a volume that would be inexpensive, easily readable and compact as possible. To accomplish this, though keeping intact all the essentials, we took the liberty of condensing many passages.

We express our deepest gratitude first to Almighty God and to His Blessed Mother for the wonderful privilege that was ours of participating in this holy crusade. We thank the Most Reverend Bishop of Leiria, Portugal, for his valuable help in so many ways and Sister Maria das Dores for her Memoirs and her constant prayers. We thank good Father John de Marchi, I.M.C. for making his book available to us and Father John Venancio, D.D., for his gracious assistance in interpreting many passages; nor can we forget the kind encouragement of the Reverend Adriano Moniz, D.D., pastor of Our Lady of Angels Church, Fall River, Mass., and the Reverend Thomas A. Steiner, C.S.C., Provincial of the Holy Cross Fathers, Notre Dame, Indiana. We are truly grateful also to P. J. Kenedy & Sons, publishers of this volume, and many others who wish their names known only to God and Mary.

May this book serve to draw the authors and all who read it closer to the Hearts of Jesus and Mary.

ASDRUBAL CASTELLO BRANCO
Our Lady of Angels Rectory
Fall River, Mass.

PHILIP C. M. KELLY, C.S.C.
Holy Cross Mission House
North Easton, Mass.

Contents

Preface to the American Edition	vii
Translators' Foreword	ix
I. The Angel	1
II. The Children of Fátima	7
III. First Apparition	11
IV. Second Apparition	26
V. Third Apparition	42
VI. Sacrifices and Sufferings	49
VII. Fourth Apparition	57
VIII. Fifth Apparition	77
IX. Sixth Apparition	87
X. Sixth Apparition (continued)	98
XI. Francisco Leads the Way	109
XII. Jacinta's Death	122
XIII. The Chapel at the Cova da Iria	143
XIV. Lúcia's Mission	147
Appendix I. Father Formigão's First Interview	162
Appendix II. Father Jongen's Interview	168
Appendix III. Filomena Miranda's Interview	172
Bibliography	176

I. The Angel

FÁTIMA is a village in the very center of Portugal,
about 70 miles north of Lisbon. It consists of numerous little hamlets hidden away in the elevation
known as Serra de Aire. One such hamlet is known
as Aljustrel; and it is here, and more especially in
the surrounding rocky pasturelands, that our story is
centered.

On a day unnamed in any of the records, in the
year 1915, four little girls had been playing in the
fields. Lúcia de Jesús dos Santos, a child of eight,
was among them. When the sun told them that it
was mid-day, they sat down to their lunch, and having finished, began the Rosary as was their custom
even at that tender age. During the recitation all
of them noticed the sudden appearance of a cloud
in form like that of a man, hovering above the foliage of the valley.

"Like a cloud, whiter than snow, slightly transparent, with a human outline," was Lúcia's description.

The little girls were surprised and filled with wonderment. They could not understand it. They were
surprised even more, when the strange white figure
appeared twice again to them. He was not paying
now merely a passing visit for he left an inexplicable
impression on their minds. Although the impression
remained with them for a long while, it diminished
with time. Perhaps, but for the events that followed,
it would have been completely forgotten.

A year passed. Lúcia as usual was out in the fields
with the sheep. This time, her little cousins, Jacinta
and Francisco were her companions and playmates.

"We had gone with the sheep to the section of my

1

father's land that lies at the foot of the Cabeço,"[1] Lúcia recalled, giving us from memory the exact details. "It is called the Chousa Velha. About mid-morning, a drizzle began to fall. Seeking shelter, we climbed the slope, followed by our sheep. It was then that we first entered the Cave that was to become so sacred. It lies in the middle of one of my god-father's olive orchards and from it can be seen the little village where I was born, my father's house and the hamlets of Casa Velha and Eira da Pedra. The olive orchards extend for long distances, until they seem to become one with these small hamlets.

"The rain stopped," Lúcia went on, "and the sun shone brightly, but we spent the day in the cave. We had our lunch and after the Rosary we started to play jacks.

"We played only a short while, when a strong wind shook the trees, and made us raise our eyes to see what was happening, for the day was serene. There above the trees toward the East, we began to see a light, whiter than snow. It was the form of a young man, transparent, more brilliant than a crystal pierced by the rays of the sun . . ." Lúcia tried to describe each detail of his appearance. "As he approached, we began to distinguish his features. We were so surprised and half absorbed, and we could not utter one word. He came near us and said:

" 'Fear not! I am the Angel of Peace. Pray with me!' "

The Angel knelt on the ground and bowed very low. By some inspiration, they imitated him and repeated the words they heard him pronounce:

"My God, I believe, I adore, I hope, and I love You. I beg pardon of You for those who do not be-

[1] "The Head," a rocky elevation some 60 feet high.

2

*lieve, do not adore, do not hope, and do not love
You."* He repeated this prayer three times. Then
he arose and said:

*"Pray this way. The Hearts of Jesus and Mary
are attentive to the voice of your supplications."*

The Angel disappeared and the awareness of the
supernatural was so intense that for a long space of
time they remained there in the same position in
which he left them, unaware of their very existence,
repeating that same prayer over and over again.

"We felt the presence of God so intensely, so inti-
mately, that we dared not speak even to each other.
The next day we felt ourselves still enveloped by
that atmosphere. Only very gradually did its inten-
sity diminish within us. None of us thought of
speaking of this apparition or of recommending that
it be kept a secret. It imposed secrecy of itself. It
was so intimate that it was not easy to utter even
a single word about it. Perhaps it made a deeper
impression upon us because it was the Angel's first
clear manifestation."

Children being children, the spell did wear off
and it was not long before they went back to their
daily round of playing, singing and dancing. One
notable effect remained, however, which seemed to
fit in with the events that followed. The three little
cousins were content to spend all their time together.

When the summer months came, bringing with
them the scorching heat of the sun, the children
were awakened each dawn to take their sheep out
to the fields while the grass was still covered with
the morning's dew. When the heat burned off the
dew, and the sheep's hunger was dulled, the children
led them back again to the barn to stay there until
evening, when they would again be led out to the

fields. Meanwhile, the three cousins spent their days playing their games under the inviting shade of the fig trees. When they were tired, they relaxed at the well, under the lacy foliage of the olive and almond trees. It was while resting there, during one early afternoon, that the Angel visited them again. Lúcia tells us what happened:

"What are you doing?" The Angel suddenly appeared at their side.

"Pray! Pray a great deal! The hearts of Jesus and Mary have designs of mercy for you! Offer unceasingly to the Most High prayers and sacrifices!"

"But how are we to sacrifice ourselves?" Lúcia said.

"Offer up everything within your power as a sacrifice to the Lord in an act of reparation for the sins by which He is offended; and of supplication for the conversion of sinners. Thus invoke peace upon our country. I am her Guardian Angel; the Angel of Portugal. Above all, accept and bear with submission the sufferings that the Lord may send you."

Only Lúcia and Jacinta heard the Angel's words. Francisco only saw the Angel and knew that he was speaking to the girls. Burning with curiosity, he wanted to learn what was said.

"Jacinta, tell me what the Angel said!"

"I will tell you tomorrow, Francisco. I am not able to speak now." The little girl was so overwhelmed, she lacked the strength to talk.

The next day as soon as he got up Francisco asked Jacinta, "Could you sleep last night? I was thinking of the Angel all night long, trying to guess what he said to you."

Lúcia told him all the Angel said. The little lad

4

could not grasp the meaning of the words of the Angel and kept interrupting, "What is the Most High? What does he mean, 'The hearts of Jesus and Mary are attentive to the voice of your supplications?' "

"When he learned the answers, he became thoughtful," Lúcia relates, "and then again started asking other questions. But my spirit was not yet entirely free. I told him to wait for the next day.

"Satisfied, he waited for a while, but he did not miss the first opportunity to ask new questions. It made Jacinta raise her voice, saying, 'Take care! We must not speak much about these matters.' "

"Every time we spoke of the Angel," says Lúcia, "I did not know what came over us. Jacinta used to say, 'I don't know what happens to me, but I cannot speak, play or sing; I don't have the strength for the smallest thing,' and Francisco would remark, 'Neither can I. What does it matter? The Angel is more important. Let us think about him.' "

In later years, Lúcia revealed: "The words of the Angel were like a light that made us realize who God was, how He loved us and wanted to be loved; the value of sacrifice, to what degree it pleased Him, and how it was rewarded with the conversion of sinners. From that moment, we began to offer to the Lord everything that mortified us, without trying to find any other ways of mortification or penance than passing hour after hour, bowed to the ground, repeating the prayer that the Angel had taught us."

Autumn drew near. The children set out with the sheep to the hills for the whole day. They were due for another surprise visit.

"We wandered from Pregueira to Lapa, going

around the hill by the side of Aljustrel and Casa Velha," Lúcia continued her report. "We said the Rosary there and the prayer that the Angel had taught us in the first apparition. Then the Angel appeared to us for the third time. He was holding a chalice in his hand. A Host was over it, from which fell some drops of Blood into the chalice. Leaving the chalice and Host suspended in mid-air, he prostrated himself on the ground, repeating this prayer three times:

" 'Most Holy Trinity, Father, Son, and Holy Ghost, I adore You profoundly, and I offer You the Most Precious Body, Blood, Soul, and Divinity of Jesus Christ, present in all tabernacles of the earth, in reparation for the outrages, sacrileges and indifferences by which He Himself is offended. And by the infinite merits of His Most Sacred Heart and the Immaculate Heart of Mary, I beg of You the conversion of poor sinners.' "

The Angel then arose, and holding the chalice and the Host again, he gave the Host to Lúcia, and the contents of the chalice to Jacinta and Francisco, while he said:

"Take and drink the Body and Blood of Jesus Christ, horribly outraged by ungrateful men. Make reparation for their crimes and console your God."

He prostrated himself again on the ground and again repeated with the children three times the prayer: "Most Holy Trinity . . ." Then he disappeared.

The full meaning of this vision unfolded slowly and astonishingly to their young minds. Their whole being became absorbed by a new, strange, yet happy feeling of the inward presence of God. They kept silence for some time. Francisco was the first

6

to break it. He had not heard the Angel speak and was anxious to learn everything.

"Lúcia," he said, "I know that the Angel gave you Holy Communion. But what did he give to me and Jacinta?"

"The same; it was Holy Communion," Jacinta replied at once, overflowing with joy, "did you not see that it was the Blood that dropped from the Host?"

"I felt that God was within me," he agreed, "but I did not know how."

The three of them remained kneeling on the ground for a long while, repeating over and over again the inspired, heart-stirring prayer of the Angel.

II. *The Children of Fátima*

THE ELDEST of the three children to whom Our Lady was to appear at Fátima was Lúcia de Jesús dos Santos. Born on March 22, 1907, she was the youngest of the seven children of Senhor Antonio dos Santos and his wife, Maria Rosa. They lived in the hamlet of Aljustrel, which is situated as an oasis among the rocky hills of Aire, forming a part of the village of Fátima. Senhor Santos was a farmer whose small holdings were scattered about the hills of the vicinity.

Lúcia was always healthy and strong. Although her features, a rather flat nose and a heavy mouth, suggested a frown, her sweet disposition and keen mind were reflected in a pair of dark, beautiful eyes which glistened under their heavy lids, making her

7

most attractive. She was particularly affectionate towards children and very early began to prove herself a help to mothers in minding their young ones. She was singularly gifted in holding the attention of the other children by her affection and resourcefulness. She is remembered also as being fond of dressing up. At the numerous religious festivals she was always among the most colorfully dressed of the girls. Moreover she loved these occasions for their gaiety, and especially for the dancing.

Lúcia's father was like many a man of his class. He did his work, performed his religious duties, and spent his free time among his friends at the tavern, leaving the children completely in the care of his wife. And she was in every way equal to the task, even if perhaps a little strict in her discipline.

Devoutly religious, Senhora Maria Rosa was possessed of more than average common sense, and, unlike most of her neighbors, she could read. Thus she was able to instruct not only her own but her neighbors' children in the catechism. Evenings she would read to the children from the Bible or other pious books, and sedulously she reminded them of their prayers, urging them particularly to remember the Rosary, traditionally the favorite devotion of the people of Portugal. It should not be surprising, therefore, that Lúcia was able to receive her First Holy Communion at the age of six instead of ten, as the custom then dictated.

Francisco and Jacinta, the other two principals, were Lúcia's first cousins, the eighth and ninth children, respectively, born of the marriage of Senhor Manuel Marto and Senhora Olimpia Jesus dos Santos. This marriage was the second for Olimpia, her first husband having died after giving her two children. Olimpia was the sister of Senhor Santos, Lúcia's father.

Francisco, their youngest boy, was born June 11, 1908. He grew to be a fine looking lad, in disposition much like his father, Ti Marto, as the parent was usually called. Lúcia recalls particularly how calm and condescending Francisco was in contrast to the whimsical and light-hearted Jacinta. Though he loved to play games, it mattered little to him whether he won or lost. In fact there were times when Lúcia shunned his company because his apparent lack of temperament irritated her. At these times she would exert her will over him, making him sit still by himself for a spell; then feeling sorry for him she would bring him into the game they might be playing, and Francisco would remain apparently unaffected by the treatment.

"Yet for all this," his father recalls, "he was sometimes wilder and more active than his sister Jacinta. He could lose his patience and fuss like a young calf. He was absolutely fearless. He would go anywhere in the dark. He would play with lizards, and when he found a small snake he made it coil itself around his staff and he filled the holes in the rocks with ewe's milk for the snakes to drink . . ."

Ti Marto, though illiterate, was a man of real wisdom and prudence. He had a remarkable sense of values, and he must have instilled into the mind and heart of Francisco a deep appreciation of the natural beauties of life. Young as the boy was he loved to contemplate the world around him; the vastness of the skies, the wonder of the stars, and the myriad beauties of nature at sunrise and sunset. Francisco loved music too. He used to carry a reed flute with which he would accompany the singing and dancing of his companions, his sister Jacinta and his cousin Lúcia.

Jacinta, born March 11, 1910, was nearly two years younger than her brother. She resembled Francisco in features, but differed sharply in temperament. Her round face was smooth-skinned, and she had bright, clear eyes and a small mouth with thin lips, but a somewhat chubby chin. She was well proportioned, but not as robust as Francisco. A quiet untroublesome infant, she grew to be a lovable child, though not without an early tendency to selfishness. She took easily to a sense of piety, but was equally given to play. In fact it seems to have been her idea sometime before the apparitions to reduce their daily Rosary to a repetition of only the first two words of the *Hail Mary,* a practice which, of course, they hastily abandoned in due time.

Jacinta had a strong devotion to Lúcia, and when it became the latter's chore to take the sheep to the hills to graze, Jacinta pestered her mother until she was given a few sheep of her own so that she could accompany her cousin to the hills. Each morning before sunrise Senhora Olimpia would awaken Francisco and Jacinta. They would bless themselves as they got up and say a little prayer. Their mother, having prepared breakfast, usually a bowl of soup and some bread, would go to the barn to release the sheep, and then, returning to the house, would prepare a lunch with whatever was at hand, probably bread with olives, codfish or sardines. By the time she had finished this, the children were ready to go to meet Lúcia with her flock of sheep. Before the apparitions they used to meet with other children, but after the apparitions of the Angel these three stayed more or less by themselves.

Lúcia would select the place for the day's pasturing. Usually they went to the wasteland, where Senhor dos Santos owned some property. Sometimes she took them out to the open country around Fátima. A favorite place in the Summer, however, was the Cabeço, a grassy hill that also offered the shade of trees—olive, pine, and holmoak—as well as the Cave. It was much closer to home than the other pasturelands, and the children found it best for playing.

One of Lúcia's earlier companions recalls, "Lúcia was a lot of fun and we loved to be with her because she was always so pleasant. We did whatever she told us to do. She was very wise, and she could sing and dance very well; and with her we could spend our whole day singing and dancing . . ." And Lúcia remembers even today all their beautiful, simple songs. When they heard the sound of the church bells, or when the height of the sun told them it was noon, they stopped their playing and dancing to recite the Angelus. After eating their lunch they would say their Rosary and then go on with their playing. They would return home in the evening in time for supper, and after their night prayers they would go to bed.

III. First Apparition

MAY, THE MONTH OF FLOWERS, follows the long April rains that wash the face of mother earth after

her long winter sleep. Then God covers the world
with jewels more beautiful than any precious stones.
What can be more beautiful than the dainty, many-
colored flowers of May?

On Sunday, the thirteenth of May, in the year
1917, during the midst of the First World War, God
sent to earth the loveliest flower of the ages, His
own beautiful Mother, Mary, whom we address as
Queen of the May. On that day the children went
to early Mass. "Heaven forbid," Senhora Marto
said, "that we should ever miss hearing Mass on
Sundays, whether it rained or thundered or even if
I were nursing my babies. Sometimes we had to
go to Boleiros, Atouguia or Santa Catarina, almost
six miles journey. I had to get up early and leave
everything in my husband's care. He would go to a
later Mass. We could not take the babies with us
when they were little, for then, neither we nor
anyone else in church would have been able to hear
Mass. Babies look like angels, but they don't act like
Angels." Returning from Mass, the mother packed
the children's lunches and sent them off with the
sheep.

This day Lúcia and her little cousins met as usual
at the small bog, beyond the village, called the
Barreiro, on the way to Gouveia, whence they proceeded to the Cova da Iria. Because the ground was
rocky and filled with so much brush, they crossed
it very slowly. It was almost noon before they
reached their chosen spot. When they heard the
church bells summoning the people to the last
Mass they knew it was time for lunch. So they
opened their bags and ate, as usual saving a little
for later on. Their meal finished, they sped through
their Rosary and then chased the sheep up the hill.

12

Their game today would be building, making castles out of the rocks. Francisco was the mason and architect, Lúcia and Jacinta gathered the stones.

While they were thus busily intent upon their building projects, a sudden bright shaft of light pierced the air. In their efforts to describe it they called it a flash [2] of lightning. Frightened,[3] they dropped their stones, looked first at each other, then at the sky which was clear and bright without the least spot of a cloud. No breeze stirred the air, the sun was shining strong. Such perfect weather belied this flash of lightning, the forerunner of a storm. The children decided that they had better start for home before it rained. Quickly they gathered the sheep and started down the hill. Half way down, just as they were passing a tall oak tree, another shaft of light split the air. Panicky with fear, and as if led by some unknown power, they took a few steps, turned towards the right, and there, standing over the foliage of a small holmoak [4] they saw a most beautiful lady.

"It was a lady dressed all in white," Lúcia records, "more brilliant than the sun, shedding rays

[2] "It was not really lightning but the reflection of a light which approached little by little. In this light, we could see Our Lady only when she was above the holmoak. We could not explain the fact to ourselves and to avoid questioning was the reason that we sometimes said that we saw Our Lady coming, sometimes not. When we said that we saw her coming, we were speaking of this light that we saw approaching which was afterward the Lady herself. When we said we had not seen it come, we meant that we saw the Blessed Virgin only when she was over the holmoak." (*Memoirs of Lúcia.*)

[3] The fear which we experienced did not properly have to do with the Blessed Virgin but rather with the storm which we believed imminent and which we wished to escape. The apparition of Our Lady inspired neither fear nor dread but only surprise." (*Memoirs of Lúcia.*)

[4] Two kinds of oak grow in Portugal, the azinheira and the carrasqueira. The azinheira is the *Quercus ilex*, famous in classical literature. It is one of the most ornamental oaks,

of light, clearer and stronger than a crystal glass filled with the most sparkling water, pierced by the burning rays of the sun."

"*Fear not!*" the Lady said, "*I will not harm you.*"

"Where are you from?" Lúcia made bold to ask.

"*I am from Heaven,*" the beautiful Lady replied, gently raising her hand towards the distant horizons.

"What do you want of me?" Lúcia humbly asked.

"*I came to ask you to come here for six consecutive months, on the thirteenth day, at this same hour. I will tell you later who I am and what I want. And I shall return here again a seventh time.*"

"And I, am I, too, going to go to Heaven?" Lúcia asked.

"*Yes, you shall,*" the Lady assured her.

"And Jacinta?"

"*Yes.*"

"And Francisco?"

"*He too shall go, but he must say many Rosaries,*" the Lady responded.

We who see things with worldly eyes are impressed only with serious faults; we forget that before God, the slightest fault is a serious matter. Though Francisco, like Lúcia and Jacinta, was immersed in the glorious light of the splendor that shone from the Lady, he was not seeing the Lady. Neither could he hear the Lady's voice, though he could hear Lúcia talking.

"I don't see anything, Lúcia! Throw a stone at it to see if it is real!" Francisco suggested.

---

compact and regular in form, beautiful in its glossy foliage the year round. Its acorns form one of the edible sorts in Europe. The carrasqueira is the *Quercus coccifera.* It is a small evergreen about three feet high, with glossy and sharp foliage, and does not give acorns. It was over a carrasqueira that Our Lady appeared at Fátima.

Throw a stone at the Lady? Never! Instead, Lúcia inquired of her, "So you are Our Lady and Francisco can't see you?"

"Let him say the Rosary!" the Lady answered, *"and in that way he too will see me."*

Lúcia passed on the command. Francisco quickly took his Rosary from his pocket to do as the Lady said. Before he finished the first decade, the Lady became visible to him with almost blinding splendor.

Meanwhile, Jacinta, solicitous for the Lady who had come so far, said, "Lúcia! Ask the Lady if she is hungry. We still have some bread and cheese."

Francisco, however, had other things on his mind. He was worried about the sheep. They had run down the hill and were in a neighbor's garden. It was planted with beans, potatoes and other vegetables and Francisco thought the sheep would eat the vegetables and destroy the garden. He realized the serious punishment he would get from his father if the sheep damaged other people's property. "Lúcia," he cried out, "I am going over there to chase the sheep. They are at the peas."

"Look here! It is not necessary! The Lady says that they will not eat them!"

"What do you mean—the sheep won't eat chickpeas?"

"Never mind, Francisco! The Lady knows." At these words, Francisco relaxed. He trusted the Lady. Lúcia asked some more questions of the Lady. Two girls who used to come to her house to learn sewing from her sisters had recently died. Lúcia wanted to find out about them, too.

"And Maria de Rosario, daughter of José das Neves, is she in Heaven?"

"Yes," the Lady replied.

16

"And Amelia?"

"She is still in Purgatory."

Lúcia's eyes filled with tears. How sad, that her friend Amelia was suffering in the fires of Purgatory. Then the Lady said to the children:

"Do you want to offer yourselves to God to endure all the sufferings that He may choose to send you, as an act of reparation for the sins by which He is offended and as a supplication for the conversion of sinners?"

Promptly Lúcia responded for all three, "Yes, we want to."

"Then you are going to suffer a great deal," the Lady promised, *"but the grace of God will be your comfort."*

As she pronounced these words, the Lady opened her hands and shed upon the children a highly intense light, that was as a reflex glancing from them. "This light penetrated us to the heart," Lúcia reported, "and its very recesses, and allowed us to see ourselves in God, Who was that light, more clearly than we see ourselves in a mirror. Then we were moved by an inward impulse, also communicated to us, to fall on our knees, while we repeated to ourselves:

" 'Most Holy Trinity, I adore You! My God, My God, I Love You in the Most Blessed Sacrament.' "

Again the Lady spoke to them, *"Say the Rosary every day to earn peace for the world and the end of the war."*

"She began then to elevate herself serenely," Lúcia said, "going in the direction of the East until she disappeared in the immensity of space, still surrounded by a most brilliant light that seemed to open a path for her through the myriad galaxies of stars."

The children stood riveted to the spot for some time, their eyes fastened on the skies where they last saw the Lady. Gradually they returned to themselves, and looking around for the sheep, they found them grazing upon the sparse grass under the shade of the holmoaks. They noticed that the vegetables in the garden were not even touched. They were ever so happy, and grateful to the Lady for her caring for the sheep, and thereby sparing them punishment at home; but their joy was supreme and beyond all description for having seen the exquisitely beautiful Mother of God. She was so wonderful, so lovely! They felt the same joy now as when the Angel visited them, only when the Angel came, they felt a sort of annihilation before his presence; whereas, with Our Lady, they received strength and courage. "Instead of bodily exhaustion, we felt a certain physical strength," Lúcia described her reaction. "In place of annihilation before the Divine Presence, we felt exultation and joy; in place of difficulty in speaking we felt a certain communicative enthusiasm."

The children spent the rest of the afternoon in the fields, living over and over again the short visit of Our Lady. They were so supremely happy, though mixed with deep concern. Our Lady seemed unhappy over something and they tried to fathom the meaning of her every word. Meanwhile, Francisco pressed the girls with questions to learn everything she had said. They told him everything. When they told him that Our Lady promised that he would go to Heaven, bursting with joy, he folded his hands in front of his breast and exclaimed aloud, "O My Lady, I will say all the Rosaries you want."

Lúcia thought it best for them to keep the vision secret. She was old enough to realize how incredulous people are about such things, and more, she had had previous and bitter experience when the girls who first saw the Angel spread the news through the neighborhood. Francisco and Jacinta both agreed to Lúcia's suggestion. Lúcia, however, doubted Jacinta's ability to keep it secret, for the little girl's face shone with joy and she would say every so often, *"Ai que Senhora tão bonita!* Oh, such a beautiful Lady!"

"I just know you are going to tell it to everyone," Lúcia warned Jacinta.

"Honest, I will not tell anyone," Jacinta assured her.

"You won't breathe a word, even to your mother?"

"I won't tell anyone."

"We'll keep it a secret," they all agreed.

But how could little Jacinta keep it a secret, when she had seen such a beautiful Lady.

When Lúcia reached home, she said not a word to anyone about the Heavenly Visitor. After supper and prayers, she listened to the reading from the New Testament and went right to bed. How different were things in her cousin's home! The Martos had gone to market that day to buy a pig. They were not home when Francisco and Jacinta returned from the fields. Francisco, meanwhile, busied himself in the yard but Jacinta waited at the door for her parents' arrival. She had already forgotten Lúcia's solemn warning, "Not a word, even to your mother." Jacinta never kept any secrets from her mother, and today, when the greatest thing on earth had happened, how could she keep it from her mother?

Finally, her mother and father came in sight, her mother walking ahead, the father guiding the little animal. "The child ran over to me," her mother described the scene, "took hold of me as she had never before done. 'Mother,' she burst out excitedly, 'I saw Our Lady today in the Cova da Iria.' 'My! My!' I said. 'Don't tell me. You must certainly be a good little girl to see Our Lady!'

"Sad and disappointed, she followed me into the house, insisting over and over again, 'But I did see her!' Then she began to tell me all that had happened, the flash, their fear, the light. She told me how beautiful and pretty the Lady was, how Francisco did not see her at first and wanted Lúcia to throw a stone at her, how the Lady was surrounded by a blinding light, how she had offered her some bread and cheese and how the Lady asked her to say the Rosary every day. I put no stock in her words, saying 'You are really silly. As if Our Lady would appear to a little girl like you!'

"Then I began to mix the feed for the little pig. My husband was standing by the pen, watching to see how it would get along with the other animals. After the animals were fed, he came into the house and sat by the kitchen fire to eat his supper. His brother-in-law, Antonio da Silva was with us and all my children were there. Then, with some severity, I told Jacinta to repeat this story of Our Lady at the Cova da Iria. Right away she began, with all the simplicity in the world."

" 'It was a lady so beautiful, so pretty . . . dressed in white, with a chain of gold around her neck extending down to her breast . . . her head was covered with a white mantle, yes, very white . . . I don't know but it was whiter even than milk . . . which covered her to the feet . . . all embroidered in gold . . . how beautiful! She kept her hands together, in this way.' The child rose from the stool, joined her hands at the breast, imitating the vision. 'She had beads between her fingers . . . Oh! what a beautiful Rosary she had . . . all of gold, brilliant as the stars at night, with a crucifix that was shining. The Lady spoke a lot with Lúcia, but never with me or with Francisco. I heard everything they said. Mother, it is necessary to say the Rosary every day! The Lady said this to Lúcia. She said also that she would take the three of us to Heaven, Lúcia, Francisco and me, too . . . and many other things I don't know, but Lúcia does. And when she entered into Heaven it seemed that the doors closed with such speed that her feet were almost caught outside. Heaven was so pretty . . . there were so many wild peonies.' "

Francisco confirmed the words of Jacinta. The girls in the family were most interested, but the boys all laughed at the story, echoing the words of their mother, "A good little saint you are, for Our Lady to appear to you." Antonio Silva tried to offer his explanation, "If the children saw a lady all dressed in white . . . who could it be but Our Lady?"

The father, meanwhile, was mulling it over in his mind, trying to fit together the religious principles involved. Finally he said, "Since the beginning of time, Our Lady has appeared many times and in many ways. This is what has been helping us. If the world is in bad shape today, it would be worse, had

21

there not been cases of this sort. The power of God is great! We do not yet know what it is, but it will be something . . . God's will be done." Later he confessed, "I believed what the children said was true almost at once. Yes, I believed immediately. For I was thinking that the children had received no education, not the least. Were it not for the help of Providence, they would never even have thought of it. Did I think the children might be lying? Not at all! Francisco and Jacinta were too much opposed to untruths." Some time later, when the Bishop of Leiria published his official decision on the matter, he did no more than develop the arguments advanced by Ti Marto over his bowl of soup. Finally, they all retired, taking the father's advice that they should leave it in God's hands.

When Jacinta's mother saw next morning some of her neighbors, she related with a smiling condescension the children's secrets. The news caused such a sensation that in no time at all it spread all through the village, finally reaching Lúcia's family.

Maria dos Anjos was the first to hear the news. "Lúcia," she said to her sister, "I have heard people talking, saying that you saw Our Lady at the Cova da Iria. Is that true?"

"Who told you?" Lúcia was so surprised that the news had gotten out. She stood there, thinking. Then, after a while, she mumbled, "And I had asked her so much not to tell anyone!"

"Why?"

"I don't know if it is Our Lady. It was a most beautiful Lady."

"And what did that Lady tell you?"

"She wanted us to go to the Cova da Iria for six

22

months, without interruption, and then she would say who she is and what she wants."

"Didn't you ask her who she was?"

"I asked her where she was from; and she said to me, 'I am from Heaven.'"

Lúcia fell into great silence so that she would not have to tell anything, but Maria coaxed her so much that she told her more. Lúcia was very sad. At this point Francisco came along and confirmed Lúcia's suspicion that it was Jacinta who had wagged her tongue. Senhora Maria Rosa laughed at the whole thing. But when her eldest daughter told her what Lúcia had said, she realized something serious was taking place. Calling Lúcia immediately, she made her repeat the whole story. The gossip is true! She hated to believe it, but it was beginning to appear that her child was turning out to be a liar!

The afternoon of the fourteenth, the children went out as usual with their sheep. Lúcia, frightened as she was by her mother's unbelieving attitude, walked along in silence. Jacinta, too, was miserable, embarrassed because she had broken her promise to Lúcia. The joy of the vision had been quickly destroyed by the ridicule and disbelief that had met their sincere account of the vision. Finally, they reached the Cova da Iria, and Jacinta sat on a rock, silent, gloomy as could be. Lúcia, feeling sorry at her little cousin's grief, forced a smile and said, "Jacinta, let's play."

"I don't want to play today!"

"Why?"

"Because I am thinking that the Lady told us to say the Rosary and make sacrifices for the conversion of sinners. Now, when we say the Rosary, we have to say every word in the *Hail Mary* and the *Our Father*."

"Yes," Lúcia agreed, "but how are we going to make sacrifices?"

"We can give our lunch to the sheep," Francisco suggested.

When noon came, they did give their lunches to the sheep. Hungry as they were, it was a hard thing to do, to give away the bread and cheese that their mothers had prepared for them. As the days went by, they thought it would be more pleasing to the Lady to give their lunches to some poor children instead of the sheep. When they themselves got hungry, Francisco climbed the holmoaks and picked acorns, even though they were still green. But this wasn't enough of a sacrifice for Jacinta. She suggested that they should prefer the acorns from the oak trees, for they were more bitter.

"That first afternoon," Lúcia recalled, "we relished this delicious meal. Other times, we ate pine seeds, roots of bell-flowers (a little yellow flower on whose root grows a little ball the size of an olive), mulberries, mushrooms and some things that we picked from the roots of pine trees, but I don't remember what they are called. We did have some fruit, if we happened to be near our parents' property."

Those days were long days for the children, for there was no song or peace of mind to help speed the hours away. Their greatest trial came from their families. Lúcia's lot was the worst. Mother, sisters, friends and neighbors, all heaped abuse upon the little one. Her father, however, refused to let the affair bother him. He shrugged his shoulders and called it just some more women's gossip. Yet if he

24

was indifferent, Lúcia's mother worried a great deal about it. She used to say, "And I was the one to be burdened with these things. This was all I needed for my old age. To think that I was always so careful to bring up my children to tell the truth, and now that girl comes up with such a lie."

Nor did Senhora Maria Rosa content herself with mere talk. She took action to stop this carrying-on of her child. One day before Lúcia went out with the sheep, her mother tried to force her to confess that she was lying. She tried caresses, threats, then resorted to the broomstick. Lúcia's answer was either silence or continued confirmation of what she had already told. Finally, in desperation, the mother commanded her, "Take the sheep out and think over during the day that I have never approved lying in my children, much less will I overlook such a lie as this. When you return in the evening, I will force you to meet those whom you deceived,—confess to them that you have lied and you will ask for their forgiveness." Lúcia went away with the sheep, and when her companions saw her coming, for they had been waiting for her, they noticed she was crying. They ran to meet her. She told them what had happened and asked for their advice. "Mother wants me to say that I lied. How can I say that? What am I going to do?"

"It's all your fault," Francisco said to Jacinta. "What did you tell it for?"

Jacinta fell on her knees crying, and stretching out her arms, begged to be forgiven. "It's all my fault, but never again will I tell anybody else."

In the evening Lúcia's mother sought again to obtain a confession, so she decided to take her to the Pastor. "When you get there," she scowled at

Lúcia, "you fall on your knees before the priest,—tell him that you lied and ask to be forgiven. Do you hear? I don't care what you think. Either you clear things up now, admit that you lied, or I will lock you in a room where you won't ever again see the light of day. I have always succeeded in having my children tell the truth before. Am I going to let a thing of this sort pass in my youngest child? If only it wasn't such an important matter!" But how could the child say that she had not seen what she did see? The words of the Lady were proving true; "You are going to suffer a great deal. But the grace of God will be your comfort."

IV. *Second Apparition*

JUNE THE THIRTEENTH was approaching, the important day when the Lady from Heaven was to appear a second time. The news of the apparition had spread all through the countryside. Everyone had his own idea on the matter; some believed, most did not. In fact, both the children and their parents were ridiculed by their neighbors. The parents were called simple-minded, unfit to bring up children or else too timid to punish them as they deserved. "I wish she were my daughter," one man said, twisting his stocking hat in his hands. "A good thrashing would soon put an end to their visions," another said, swinging his staff. Even the other children jeered and scoffed when Lúcia and her cousins passed them.

Meanwhile, Lúcia's mother, in her good faith,

went to consult with the village Pastor, the Reverend Manuel Marques Ferreira. After hearing the mother's version, he suggested that the children be allowed to return to the Cova da Iria on the following thirteenth and that they be brought to him afterwards. He would interrogate them individually. Going home, Senhora Santos met Ti Marto and told him of the Pastor's advice. He thought it wise to go and talk it over with the Pastor also. When he reached the rectory, and was taken into the house, he said, "Senhor Prior, my sister-in-law has just told me that you want me to come here with the children after the next apparition, one at a time. I have come now to find out the best thing for us to do."

"What a mess this is," the Pastor remarked; "sometimes it is white, sometimes it is black."

"But, Reverend Father, you seem more ready to believe lies than facts," Ti Marto answered calmly.

"So far, I have never had to listen to anything of this sort," the Pastor countered, noticeably vexed by the whole affair. "Everybody knows things before me. If you want to bring the children to me, do it; if not, don't bring them."

"Senhor Prior, I have come with nothing but the best intentions in mind."

Ti Marto then got up to leave, but as he descended the stairs of the veranda, he could still hear the Pastor repeating, "Ti Marto, I leave it to you. If you want to bring them, do it; if not, don't bring them."

"Good Father, I have come only to find out what is best for us to do, not to cause any trouble."

Among those few who did believe, there is one who deserves special mention, Senhora Maria Carreira. Later, she came to be known as Maria da

Capelinha (the Lady of the Little Chapel). In her room in the hospital at the Shrine of Fátima, she told the author all she knew about the great happenings at the Cova da Iria, of which she had been a witness almost from the very beginning. "I had always been sick," she said, "and those seven years before the apparitions, the doctors gave me up completely. They said I had only a short time to live." Two or three days after the first apparition, Senhora Carreira's husband had been working with Lúcia's father, and Antonio dos Santos told him about his daughter.

That night, Senhor Manuel Carreira said to Maria, his wife, "My dear, Antonio dos Santos told me that Our Lady appeared to one of his girls, the youngest one, and to two of the children of his sister, the one married to Francisco Marto. Our Lady spoke to them and promised to return there every month through October."

Maria da Capelinha's curiosity was aroused. "I'm going to find out if this is true. If it is, I want to go there. Where is the Cova da Iria?"

Her husband told her, and although it was only a ten minute walk from their house, she had never gone there before. One never spoke of the place before. Senhor Carreira tried to discourage her from going. "You must be a fool. Do you think you too will see Our Lady?"

"I know I won't see her, but if we heard that the king was going there, we wouldn't stay at home. If they say that Our Lady is coming, why shouldn't I go and at least try to see her?" Later this lady was to be a great comfort to the little children through her kind understanding and helpful assistance.

28

The great feast of St. Anthony was approaching. Excitement rode high in the parish; everyone, old and young, was preparing for the celebration of the feast which also fell on the thirteenth. While the bells rang, oxcarts trimmed with branches, flowers, flags and draperies, and laden with five hundred bread-rolls, would be led around the church a few times before stopping under the Pastor's balcony for the blessing of the gifts. Maria Rosa knew how her youngest daughter liked celebrations, and she hoped this festival would help her forget about the Cova da Iria. "How good that tomorrow is our feast day," she said to her daughters. "We will be talking of nothing but the feast. We ourselves are to blame, always reminding Lúcia of the Cova."

The family tried to avoid the problem of the apparition. When Lúcia did bring it up, they changed the subject to divert her mind and make her forget her plans. Lúcia took this for disdain and contempt on her family's part; she felt they had abandoned her. Lonely and sorrowful, she became very quiet, but every once in a while she blurted out, "Tomorrow, I am going to the Cova da Iria. It is what the Lady wants."

In spite of the Pastor's advice to allow the children to go to the Cova on the thirteenth of June, both mothers wished to prevent their going. Jacinta wished so very much to share with her mother the joy of the vision, but her mother would not believe it at all. Overcome with enthusiasm for the cause of Our Lady, Jacinta pleaded, "Mamma, come with us tomorrow to see Our Lady."

"Our Lady! What do you mean, silly little girl? No! Tomorrow, we go to the feast. Don't you want to get your roll? Besides, there is the band, and rockets and a special sermon." The mother thought the mention of the band and the rolls would surely make the child forget about the Cova; little did she realize that music and food no longer attracted her child. For a month now the little children had given up singing and dancing, even their lunches, for the conversion of sinners.

"But mother, Our Lady does appear at the Cova da Iria."

"Our Lady does not appear to you, so it is useless to go there," Senhora Marto contradicted her child.

"Oh, but she does. Our Lady said that she would appear and she will," Jacinta rejoined.

"Don't you want to go to the feast?" Senhora Marto tried to change the subject.

"Saint Anthony is not beautiful."

"Why?"

"Because the Lady is more, much more beautiful. I am going to the Cova da Iria. If the Lady tells us to go to the feast of Saint Anthony, then we'll go."

Jacinta's father, Ti Marto, was in the same predicament. He didn't know what to do on the feast day. Should he go to the Cova? But what if nothing appeared? It didn't seem right that he should go to the celebration at the church and let the children go alone to the Cova. Finally he decided, since it was market day in Pedreira, he would go there instead, buy the oxen he wanted, and when he returned, everything would have been settled. Yes, that's it; he would go to market. That would save him committing himself. He went to sleep in peace.

As soon as Jacinta awakened in the morning, she ran into her mother's room to invite her again to come to see the Lady. But her mother's room was empty, and Jacinta was sorely disappointed. "Mother will not see Our Lady today," she said. Then she thought to herself, "But at least now we can go in peace." She awakened Francisco, and while he dressed, she let out the sheep. As soon as Francisco was ready, they hurried away to meet Lúcia, nibbling on some bread and cheese as they went.

Lúcia was already waiting for them at the Barreiro. So bitter did she feel at the lack of understanding and the cruel opposition of her mother and sisters that she was impatient to be alone with her cousins. Only with them did she feel joyful and happy. They alone understood and believed in her as she understood and believed in them. In her memoirs she writes, "I recalled the times that were past and I asked myself, where was the affection which my family had had for me only a short while ago."

But the Lady was coming, they had no time to lose. They must make sure to be at the Cova on time. "Today, let's go to Valinhos," Lúcia decided. "There is plenty of grass there and the sheep will get through fast. Then we can go home and put on our best clothes. I won't wait for you, because I want to go to Fátima to talk with some of the girls who made their First Communion with me."

Later, when Lúcia's mother saw her child getting all dressed up, she rubbed her hands with satisfaction at the thought that Saint Anthony had answered her prayer that Lúcia might forget the whole thing. They watched to see where Lúcia was going. To Fátima or the Cova da Iria. If Lúcia went to the Cova, her mother decided that she had better follow her. She would hide herself so she could watch what went on and see if the girl were lying. Also she wanted to be there lest anyone try to harm the children. She wasn't going to let anyone hurt her Lúcia, nor would she allow Lúcia to fall into the bad habit of lying.

All worried and excited, she decided she had better go to the church first. On the way, she met some strangers who, she presumed, were going to attend the feast. She called to them, "Look here, you're going the wrong way. That's not the way to Fátima."

"We just came from Fátima. We're going to see the children who saw Our Lady."

"Where are you from?" she inquired.

"From Carrascos. Where are the children?"

"They are in Aljustrel, but they'll soon be coming to the feast."

Meanwhile, Lúcia found her way to church, saw her First Communion friends and invited them to come to the Cova da Iria with her. Usually whenever Lúcia suggested something her friends concurred, so altogether fourteen girls agreed to go along. While they were walking towards the Cova da Iria Lúcia's brother, Antonio, tried to stop them; he even offered a bribe of a few pennies. "I don't care for your pennies," Lúcia cried out. "All I want is to go to the Cova da Iria." He followed the girls for a while, urging them to come back, but soon gave up the attempt.

The fourteen girls were not alone at the Cova. A few people had joined them on the way and when they reached the place where the gate to the shrine is now situated, they were met by a small group of women, among whom were Maria da Capelinha and her crippled seventeen year old son. Senhora da Capelinha describes the happenings of this eventful day. "Being determined to go to the Cova on the thirteenth, I said to my daughters the evening before, 'Why don't we go to the Cova tomorrow instead of to the feast of Saint Anthony?'

" 'To the Cova da Iria? What for? We would rather go to the feast.'

"Turning to my crippled son, I said, 'and how about you? Do you want to go to the feast or will you go with me?'

" 'I'll go with you, mother.'

"The next day, even before the others had left for the feast," continues the lady, "I came here (to the Cova da Iria) with my son John who had to use a staff to get along. There wasn't a soul around, so we went back to the road which we knew the children would take and sat down. After a while, a woman came along from Loureira. She was very surprised to see me there, for she knew I was sick and had been confined to my bed. 'What are you here for?' she said.

" 'For the same reason that you came here.' Without another word, she sat down beside me. Then a man came along from Lomba da Égua and we exchanged about the same words. Then a few women from Boleiros came along. I asked them if they were running away from the feast.

"One woman answered, 'Some people made fun of us, but who cares? We want to see what happens here and find out whether it is they or we who should be made fun of.'

"Still others came, some from as far away as Torres Novas, and around eleven o'clock, the children arrived. We followed them until they stopped near a little holmoak tree. I asked Lúcia, 'Little girl, which is the holmoak over which Our Lady appears?'

" 'See here? It was here that she stood.' "

It was a small tree, about three feet high, being

at the peak of its growth, with straight, beautiful branches. Lúcia withdrew herself a little, turned towards Fátima, then walked over to a large holmoak and sat down against the trunk to get in the shade. The day was very hot. Francisco and Jacinta sat at her side.

While eating lupini they talked and amused themselves with the other children. But as time went by, Lúcia became more and more serious and apprehensive. Soon she said to Jacinta, who was still playing, "Quiet. Our Lady is coming."

It was near noon. Maria da Capelinha was feeling weak. "Will it be long before Our Lady comes?" she asked.

"No, Senhora," Lúcia unhesitatingly responded. They all began the Rosary, and as they finished, one girl began the Litany. But Lúcia stopped her, "There's no time for it now." Then she got up and shouted, "Jacinta, Jacinta, here comes Our Lady. I just saw the flash."

The three of them ran over to the smaller holmoak. Everyone followed and knelt upon the brush and furze. Lúcia raised her eyes towards the skies, as if in prayer, and was heard to say, "You told me to come here today. What do you want me to do?"

The others heard something that sounded like a very gentle voice but did not understand what was said. "It is like the gentle humming of a bee," Maria de Capelinha whispered.

Lúcia in later years tells us as follows:

"I want you to come here on the thirteenth of the next month. Say the Rosary, inserting between the mysteries the following ejaculation—'O My Jesus, forgive us. Save us from the fire of Hell. Bring all souls to Heaven, especially those in most need.' I

34

want you to learn to read and write and later I will tell you what else I want."

Then Lúcia asked Our Lady to cure a sick person who was recommended to her. Our Lady answered,

"If he is converted, he will be cured within the year."

"I would like to ask you also to take us to Heaven!"

"Yes," our Lady answered, *"I will take Jacinta and Francisco soon. You, however, are to stay here a longer time. Jesus wants to use you to make me known and loved. He wants to establish the Devotion to my Immaculate Heart in the world. I promise salvation to those who embrace it and their souls will be loved by God as flowers placed by myself to adorn His throne."*

"Am I going to stay here alone?" Lúcia asked, full of sadness at the thought of losing her beloved cousins.

"No, My Daughter."

Lúcia's eyes filled with tears.

"Does this cause you to suffer a great deal? I will never leave you, my Immaculate Heart will be your refuge and the way that will lead you to God."

"As she said these last words," Lúcia tells, "the Blessed Virgin opened her hands and communicated to us for the second time the reflex of the immense light that enveloped her. We saw ourselves in it, as if submerged in God. Jacinta and Francisco seemed to be on the side that was ascending to Heaven, and I was on the side that was spreading over the earth. There was a Heart before the palm of the right hand of Our Lady, with thorns piercing it. We understood that this was the Immaculate Heart of Mary, so offended by the sins of mankind, desiring reparation."

The crowd now saw Lúcia rise quickly to her feet. Stretching out her arm she cried,

"Look, there she goes; there she goes!"

Maria de Capelinha reports that when Our Lady left the tree, it was like the hissing of a distant rocket. She continues: "As for us, we saw nothing but a slight cloud, just a few inches away from the foliage, rising slowly towards the East."

The children remained silent, their eyes fastened in that direction, until a few minutes later, Lúcia cried out, "There now! It's all over. She has entered Heaven. The doors have closed."

The people turned their eyes back to the blessed holmoak and were surprised to see the highest branches, which before were standing upright, now inclined towards the east, as if they had been tread upon. The onlookers then began to break off the branches and leaves from the holmoak. Lúcia asked that they take only the lower branches, as they had not been touched by Our Lady. Someone suggested that everybody say the Rosary before leaving, but because some had come such a long way, they said only the Litany at the Cova; then departing in a group, they recited the Rosary together on their way home.

When they reached the village of Fátima, even though the procession in honor of Saint Anthony was in progress, they were immediately noticed. Of course they told everyone how happy they were for having gone to the Cova instead of remaining in the village for the feast, and many felt sorry for themselves, not having done the same.

Maria da Capelinha recalls that evening being

questioned by her daughters. "When I said that I was sorry they had not been there also, they decided to go with me next Sunday, which they did. On that occasion, while we were saying the Rosary by the holmoak, we noticed two people going by and saying, 'Look, some people are already at the place where Our Lady appeared!' We hid behind some bushes then. The people placed carnations on the holmoak and knelt to say the Rosary. Since that day then, I began going every day to the Cova da Iria. At home I always felt so weak and helpless, but as soon as I reached the Cova, I felt like a different person. I removed all the stones that were there and pulled out or cut away the thickets and furze. I gave the place the shape of a round thrashing floor. I also tied a silk ribbon on the branches of the holmoak and I was the first one to place flowers on it."

Not everyone who had been in the Cova da Iria left immediately after the Litany. Some few remained to ask the children the details of the apparition. The little ones told what they were allowed to tell, but kept the rest to themselves. About four o'clock they left for home, followed by this reverent little group of people. Passers-by made fun of them. The children did not mind it for themselves, but it seemed the people were ridiculing Our Lady. "Lúcia, has the Lady come again for a walk over the holmoaks?"

"Jacinta, didn't the Lady tell you anything this time?"

"What, you are still on earth! Haven't you gone to Heaven yet?" It was with a sigh of relief that Jacinta crossed the door into her house.

There, however, the questioning continued. Her

37

sisters asked all kinds of questions, but, made wise by past experience, Jacinta answered very cautiously. How she longed to go to her mother and tell the whole story, and that Our Lady promised to take her soon to Heaven. Yet some mysterious force made her hold her tongue. All three children felt the same obligation to silence. Jacinta, however, did feel free to speak easily about the entrancing beauty of the Lady.

"Was the Lady as beautiful as so-and-so?" her sisters asked.

"Much more beautiful!"

"Was she like the little statue in church, with the mantle of stars?"

"No, she was very much more beautiful!"

"As beautiful as Our Lady of the Rosary?"

"Much more beautiful."

Her sisters and mother began to show her pictures of all the saints they had in the parlor, but the beauty of the Lady she had seen was greater than all and could not be compared with any of them. But, they insisted, "What did the Lady tell you this time?"

Jacinta lowered her head, repeating, "She said it is necessary to say the Rosary . . . she said she will return and she told us a secret that we cannot tell."

A secret! A secret! What could it be? From that moment on, Jacinta never again had peace. Everyone tried to pry it out of her. Her good father was the only exception. "All the women wanted to know what it might be," he said, "but I never bothered her. A secret is a secret and has to be kept. I remember once that some ladies came, all decked out in their jewels. They asked Jacinta if she liked their gold chains and bracelets."

38

" 'I like them,' she admitted.

" 'Would you like to have them?'

" 'Yes.'

" 'Then tell us the secret!' and they pretended to take off the jewels. But the child was all worried and cried out, 'Don't! Don't! Take them away! I won't tell a thing. I won't tell the secret even if you gave me the whole world.' "

Another time, Maria das Neves and her niece were talking to Jacinta alone in the house. "Look here, Jacinta," the woman said, "tell me the secret and I will give you this chain of gold beads!"

"If you give me that lovely medal, hanging around your niece's neck," Jacinta playfully answered, "I'll tell you."

"Oh, but I couldn't give you that one for it's hers."

"But I'll give it to you," the niece cut in.

"I was only fooling," replied Jacinta, "I don't want it. I wouldn't tell the secret for the whole world."

The evening of the apparition, Lúcia's sisters kept after her, trying to know her secrets. Disappointed, they threatened her with all kinds of evil. They spoke of the coming session with the Pastor and the punishment if she insisted on her silence even with him. The frightened girl went over to her cousin's home to warn them. "Tomorrow we will see the priest. I am going with mother. My sisters have been trying to scare me," Lúcia said.

"We're going, too," Jacinta told her, "but mother hasn't tried to scare us with any of those things. But if they do beat us, we will suffer it for love of Our Lord and for sinners."

However, when the children next morning reached the rectory, the Pastor and his sister received them graciously. The Pastor hoped to settle his doubts. He thought that if Our Lady really appeared, she must have given the children an important message, and he felt he had a right to know it. Jacinta was the first to be questioned. She bowed her head before the priest in complete silence. Francisco spoke only two or three words. Lúcia, however, did tell the Pastor something of what happened.

"It is not possible that Our Lady would come down from Heaven just to tell us that the Rosary should be said every day," remarked the Pastor. "This practice is followed almost by the whole parish. As a rule, when things of this sort happen, Our Lord directs the souls that He speaks with to give a full account to their pastors or confessors. This child holds back as much as she can. This could be a trick of the devil. Time will tell us what attitude we must take."

The reticence of the children did not allow the Pastor to realize the world-wide import of the apparitions. Had Lúcia said a little more, she might have at least destroyed the Pastor's doubts and regained peace. The children and the Pastor were caught in a whirlwind. Our Lady's promise to Lúcia applied also to the Pastor, "You are going to suffer a great deal."

When Lúcia left the rectory, she was very uneasy, very worried. Is this a trick of the devil? Is the priest right? Who am I to say the priest is wrong? The child was terribly upset. "I began to doubt the manifestations then lest they might have come from the devil who wanted to destroy my soul. Since I heard that the devil always brings trouble and disorder, I began to think that, in truth, I could find neither joy nor peace in our home since I had seen

40

these things. How unhappy I was . . . I told my cousins of this doubt and Jacinta quieted me, 'Lúcia, it is not the devil! Not at all! They say that the devil is very ugly and that he is under the earth in Hell. The Lady is so beautiful and we saw her rise into Heaven.'"

Poor Lúcia could not get the doubts out of her mind. So distraught was she, that she went as far as to consider saying that it was all a lie. Jacinta and Francisco, her angels of consolation, were always at hand to strengthen her. "Don't do it!" they urged her. "Don't you see that it is now that you are going to lie and lying is a sin!"

The encouraging words of her little cousins helped clear her mind. But doubts kept coming back with increasing force. One night, Lúcia had a terrible dream. "I saw the devil laughing at me because he had deceived me, and he was struggling, trying to drag me into Hell. Seeing myself in his claws, I began to cry so loud, calling for Our Lady, that I awoke my mother. Mother answered anxiously, asking what was the matter with me. I do not remember what I told her. What I do remember is that I could not fall asleep again that night since I was numbed with fear. This dream left my soul in a cloud of anguish and terrible fear."

The only place where Lúcia could enjoy any semblance of peace was with her cousins near the holm-oak.

V. Third Apparition

THE DATE of the next apparition was approaching.
Jacinta and Francisco were the happiest children in
the world. Lúcia's heart, however, was filled with
gloom and despair; so much so, that she made up her
mind not to go to the Cova da Iria again. So often
did her mother repeat the words of the Pastor that
it was the work of the devil, that it upset her.

One day, the Pastor was talking to José Alves,
one of the first to believe in the apparitions. "It is
the invention of the devil," the priest said.

"Not at all, Father," Alves spoke up, "there is
praying at the Cova da Iria, and the devil does not
like that."

"The devil even goes to the Communion rail,"
countered the priest.

"You have studied, Father—I have not." The man
would not argue with the Pastor.

The eve of the thirteenth, Lúcia went to Jacinta
and Francisco and told them of her decision not
to go to the Cova the next day. "We are going!"
they answered her; "the Lady told us to go there."

"I will speak to her," Jacinta declared, breaking
into tears.

"Why are you crying?" Lúcia asked.

"Because you don't want to go."

"No, I am not going. Look! If the Lady asks for
me, tell her I am not going because I fear she is
the devil," and then Lúcia, grief-stricken, hurried
away. The people were already gathering for the
apparition next day and she wanted to hide herself
from them. In the evening, her mother, thinking
that Lúcia had been out playing all the time, scolded

42

her. "What a little wooden saint you are, eaten up with termites. Every minute you have away from the sheep you spend playing and no one can find you."

The morning of July thirteenth came, and Lúcia felt the same doubt and confusion. By some strange impulse, however, when it was time to leave for the Cova, every doubt and fear disappeared. Her heart was transformed. Joyfully she went to her cousins' house to see if they had gone. They were still there, both of them, kneeling by the side of the bed, crying their eyes out.

"Aren't you going?" Lúcia asked.

"Without you we didn't dare go," they said. But realizing that Lúcia had changed her mind they jumped to their feet.

"Let's go," they said together.

"I was on my way now," Lúcia responded. So, off they went, the three of them, walking happily through the crowds of people that jammed the roads to the Cova. The three children could not hurry, because many people stopped them, asking them to speak to Our Lady and ask special favors for them.

Jacinta's mother, seeing all the people going towards the Cova, was afraid. She went to Lúcia's mother, "Comadre," [5] she pleaded, "We must go to the Cova, too. We may never again see our children. What if they kill them?"

"Don't worry," Lúcia's mother responded; "if it is Our Lady who appears to them, she will defend them. If it is not, then I don't know what might happen." Together, the two mothers went to the Cova, each carrying a blessed candle which they intended to light in case it was something evil. When

[5] Comadre or co-mother; a term expressing the relationship between the natural mother of a child and the child's godmother.

they reached the place, they crouched behind the bushes, their hearts pounding in expectation of some approaching evil.

Ti Marto was thoroughly convinced of the truth of the apparitions. He knew well that the accusations made against himself, Lúcia's parents and the priests were false. The children were never known to lie and received encouragement from no one. The Pastor even supposed the visions were the work of the devil. Ti Marto made up his mind to follow his children boldly to the Cova da Iria. "With these thoughts in mind," he confessed, "I took to the road. How crowded it was! I could not catch sight of the children but from the knots of people stopping now and then and gathering together, I guessed they were going ahead. In a sense, this suited me better. However, when I got to the Cova da Iria, I could not keep myself back anymore. I wanted to be the closest one to the children. But how? I could not break through for the great crush of people. At a certain point, two men, one from Ramila and the other from our village, made a circle around the children. When they happened to see me, they pulled my arm and shouted, 'Here is their father! Come right in here!' and so I was able to stand very close to my Jacinta.

"Lúcia knelt a little ahead and was leading the Rosary, which we all answered aloud. When the Rosary was over, Lúcia stood up, looked towards the East and cried out, 'Close the umbrellas, close the umbrellas. Our Lady is coming!' Looking closely, I saw something like a small greyish cloud hovering over the holmoak. The sun turned hazy and a refreshing breeze began to blow. It did not seem that we were then at the height of summer. The silence

44

of the crowd was impressive. Then I began to hear a hum as of a gadfly within an empty jug, but did not hear a word. It seems to me that it must have been as when people speak on the phone, not that I have ever used a phone. To me, all this was great proof of the miracle."

Many years later, Lúcia gave the details of this extraordinary apparition. With the unbounded love of a mother bending over her sick child, wishing to strengthen and console the children in the truth of the apparitions, the beautiful Lady engulfed the three in her immense light and rested her loving eyes on Lúcia. The girl could not speak for joy. Jacinta prodded her, "Lúcia, go ahead, speak to her. She is already speaking to you."

So Lúcia, looking up towards Our Lady, her eyes filled with loving devotion, asked, "What do you want of me?"

"I want you to return here on the thirteenth of next month," the Lady said. *"Continue to say the Rosary every day in honor of Our Lady of the Rosary to obtain peace for the world and the end of the war; for she alone can save it."*

Lúcia, thinking of her mother and the words of the Pastor, wishing to clear up the doubts of people, spoke again in her own childish manner, "Will you please tell us who you are and perform a miracle so that everyone will believe that you really appear to us?"

"Continue to come here every month. In October, I will say who I am and what I desire and I will perform a miracle all shall see so that they believe."

Then Lúcia spoke of the petitions of the people. Our Lady answered, *"Some I will cure and others not. As to the crippled boy, I will not cure him or take him out of his poverty, but he must say the Rosary every day with his family."*

Lúcia told her of the case of a sick person who wished to be taken soon to Heaven.

"He should not try to hurry things. I know well when I shall come for him."

Lúcia asked for the conversion of some people. The answer of the Lady was, as with the crippled boy, the recitation of the Rosary. Then to remind the children of their special vocation and to inspire them to greater fervor and courage for the future, the Lady said:

"Sacrifice yourselves for sinners; and say often, especially when you make some sacrifice: 'My Jesus, it is for love of You, for the conversion of sinners, and in reparation for sins committed against the Immaculate Heart of Mary.'"

"As Our Lady said these words," Lúcia later described the scenes, "She opened her hands again as she had done the two previous months. The light reflecting from them seemed to penetrate into the earth, and we saw as if into a sea of fire, and immersed in that fire were devils and souls with human form, as if they were transparent black or bronze embers floating in the fire and swayed by the flames that issued from them along with clouds of smoke, falling upon every side just like the falling of sparks in great fires, without weight or equilibrium, amidst wailing and cries of pain and despair that horrified and shook us with terror. We could tell the devils by their horrible and nauseous figures of baleful and unknown animals, but transparent as the black coals in a fire."

Frightened, deathly pale, the little ones raised their eyes to Our Lady for help as Lúcia cried out.

46

•

"Oh, . . . Our Lady!"

Our Lady explained: *"You have seen Hell—where the souls of poor sinners go. To save them God wants to establish throughout the world the devotion to my Immaculate Heart.*

"If people will do what I will tell you, many souls will be saved, and there will be peace. The war is going to end.

"But if they do not stop offending God, another and worse war will break out in the reign of Pius XI. When you see a night illumined by an unknown light, know that it is the great sign that God gives you, that He is going to punish the world for its crimes by means of war, hunger, persecution of the Church and of the Holy Father.

"To forestall this, I shall come to ask the consecration of Russia to my Immaculate Heart and the Communion of Reparation on the First Saturdays.

"If they heed my request, Russia will be converted, and there will be peace. If not, she shall spread her errors throughout the world, promoting wars and persecutions of the Church; the good will be martyred, the Holy Father will have much to suffer, various nations will be annihilated; in the end, my Immaculate Heart shall triumph. The Holy Father will consecrate Russia to me, which will be converted, and some time of peace will be given to the world.

"In Portugal, the dogma of the faith will be kept always.

"Do not tell this to anyone. To Francisco, yes, you may tell it."

Lúcia, her heart aching to do something heroic for her Lady, once again said to her, in childlike abandon, "Don't you want anything else from me?"

47

"No; today I desire nothing else from you."

At this point something like thunder was heard, and a little arch that had been set up to hold vigil lanterns shook as if there had been an earthquake. Lúcia arose, turning around so fast that her skirt flared. "There she goes," she shouted, pointing up to Heaven, "There she goes." Then a few moments later, "She's gone!"

The small, greyish cloud vanished and as soon as the children recovered from their spell of emotions, a ruthless, inquisitive crowd surrounded them, all saying at once, "Lúcia, what did the Lady say to make you look so sad?"

"It is a secret," she responded.

"Is it something good?"

"For some, it is good; for others, it is evil."

"Won't you tell it?" they pressed.

"No, I cannot tell it," she answered with convincing determination.

The people kept pushing so much that they almost smothered the children. Jacinta's father, frightened for the safety of his children, perspiration rolling down his face from the excitement of the occasion, elbowed his way close to the children, picked up Jacinta in his strong arms and, sheltering her from the sun with his hat, started for the road home.

The two mothers, still hiding behind the bushes, felt all strength gone from them. When they saw the crowd milling around their children, Jacinta's mother cried out, "Oh, good mother, they are killing our children!" How relieved both were a few moments later to see Jacinta on the shoulders of her father, Francisco in the arms of a relative, and Lúcia being carried by a very tall man, so tall in fact that

48

Lúcia's mother was distracted from her worry. "Oh, what a big man," she blurted out.

VI. *Sacrifices and Sufferings*

AFTER THIS THIRD APPARITION of Our Lady the three children yearned more and more to be left alone to say their prayers and make their sacrifices for Our Lady; but whenever they were seen on the streets, the crowds of people gathered to ask them all sorts of questions about the apparitions. To avoid these questioners, they had to wend their way to their pastures over back roads and deserted lanes. So filled were they with the thought of pleasing the Lady that nothing else counted, neither singing nor dancing nor even the flute playing of little Francisco.

"What are you thinking about, Jacinta," Lúcia asked one morning, noticing a cloud of sadness veiling her face.

"I am thinking of Hell, and poor sinners. How sorry I am for the souls that go to Hell . . . the people there, alive, burning as wood in the fire . . . Lúcia, why is it that Our Lady does not show Hell to sinners? If they saw it, they would not commit any more sins, so they would not go there."

Lúcia, puzzled, could find no word to answer. But Jacinta insisted, "Why did you not tell Our Lady to show Hell to all those people?"

"I forgot," Lúcia admitted.

Jacinta then knelt on the ground, while she raised her folded hands towards Heaven, sighing out the prayer that the Lady taught them to say: "O My

Jesus, forgive us; save us; save us from the fire of Hell; bring all souls to Heaven, especially those in most need." Lúcia and Francisco both followed suit, kneeling as they said the Lady's prayer with Jacinta. Jacinta, however, was so engrossed in her prayer, she did not realize Lúcia was praying with her, and she spoke up, "Lúcia, Francisco, are you praying with me? We must pray a great deal to save souls from Hell. So many go there!"

The thought of Hell and the souls suffering in its fire so filled the child's mind, she could not fathom the reasons for it. "Lúcia," she went to Lúcia in all her problems, "Lúcia, what have these people done to go to Hell?"

"I don't know! Maybe they sinned by missing Mass on Sunday. Maybe they said ugly words, stole, swore . . ."

"And do they go to Hell just for one word?"

"If it is a big sin . . ."

"How easy it was for them to have held their tongues or go to Mass! How sorry I am for them! If I could only show them Hell . . ."

Tired and weary from kneeling so long, they got up and walked to the shade of the large holmoaks to think some more on the words of their Lady. Francisco spoke up this time, "Why did Our Lady hold in her hand a heart, spreading upon the world that great light that is God? Lúcia, you were with Our Lady in the light that came towards the earth; but Jacinta and I in the light that went up to Heaven."

"You and Jacinta will go to Heaven soon, but I have to stay in the world longer."

"How many years?"

"I don't know, but for many."

50

"Was it the Lady who told you?"

"No, but I saw it in that light that she sent into our hearts."

"That's true," Jacinta spoke up, "I also saw it that way. I am going to Heaven but you are going to stay here. If Our Lady lets you, tell everyone what Hell is like, so that they won't sin any more. So many people falling into Hell, so many people . . ."

"You don't have to be afraid," Lúcia said, "you are going to Heaven."

"Yes, I shall go; but I want everybody to go there, too."

The cool hours of the morning gave way to the stifling heat of the day. The children burned with thirst, but there was not a drop of water near. Instead of complaining, seven year old Jacinta seemed happy. "How good it is," she said: "I am thirsty but I offer everything for the conversion of sinners."

Lúcia, the oldest of the three, realized she should look after her cousins, so she went to a nearby house to fetch some water. When she returned, she offered it first to Francisco.

"I don't want to drink," the nine year old boy said; "I want to suffer for sinners."

"Jacinta, you drink it."

"I also want to offer a sacrifice." So Lúcia poured out the water into the hollow of a rock for the sheep to drink and returned the empty jug to the house.

Francisco, however, became very weak and was almost fainting. The rhythmic noises of crickets, frogs and insects began to pound in his ears like thunder. Holding his head in his hands, he cried out in utter desperation, "My head aches so. Tell the crickets and frogs to stop."

"Don't you want to suffer this for sinners?" Lúcia asked.

"Yes, I do, Lúcia; let them sing."

"Lúcia," Jacinta interrupted, "the Lady said that her Immaculate Heart shall be your refuge and the way that shall lead you to God. Doesn't that make you happy? I love her Heart very much."

"I should like to go with you," Lúcia confessed, thinking of the beautiful joys of Heaven.

"Lúcia, don't you remember? . . . The Heart of Our Lady encircled by thorns? How pitiful! I am so sorry for her . . . She asked for the Communion of reparation, but how could I do it, if I can't receive Communion yet?"

Filled with such thoughts, the days sped by for these three children.

One time, Jacinta was alone near the well, while Lúcia and Francisco went to look for some wild honey. All at once a vision of the Pope came before her. Thinking that the others would see everything she did, she called them back, "Lúcia! Francisco! Did you see the Holy Father?"

"No."

"I don't know how it happened," Jacinta went on. "I saw the Holy Father in a very big house. He was kneeling before a table, holding his face in his hands and he was crying. Outside, there were many people; some were throwing stones at him, others were swearing at him and saying many ugly words to him. How pitiful it was! We must pray a lot for him."

Another time, while they were in the cave of the Cabeço saying the prayer of the Angel, Jacinta suddenly got up, her eyes filled with tears, "Lúcia," she sobbed, "don't you see all those roads and lanes and fields covered with people crying from hunger, without anything to eat? And the Holy Father in a church praying before the Immaculate Heart of Mary? And all those praying with him?"

As news of the apparitions spread throughout the country, the number of visitors to Fátima increased daily. Some were devout, others were merely curious; but all wanted to see the Cova da Iria and to speak to the three children. Jacinta's father tells of this in his own words.

"Many ladies came, elaborately dressed. We might be doing our chores in our everyday clothes and they embarrassed us very much. Oh, but were they curious, very, very curious. They were all after the secret. They sat Jacinta on their lap and plagued her with questions. But she answered only when it suited her. They petted her, offered her presents, but all in vain. It was a secret that could not be extracted even with a corkscrew.

"Some well-dressed gentlemen came only to laugh and make fun of us, who did not even know how to read. Very often, we were the ones who laughed last. Poor things! They had no faith. How could they believe in Our Lady? The children seemed to sense this type of person and they would vanish in the wink of an eye."

Once a car stopped at the door, a large family got out. The three children scattered over the house; Lúcia hid under the bed, Francisco climbed to the attic, but Jacinta, who was not so nimble, was caught. When the visitors left, Lúcia came out from under the bed and said to Jacinta, "What did you say when they asked for me?"

"I kept very quiet. I knew where you were, but lying is a sin."

They laughed and joked about it, their playing "hide and seek" with the visitors. "What questions the people asked!" Ti Marto continued, "Did Our Lady also have goats and sheep? Did she eat potatoes? Such foolishness!"

The priests were no less inquisitive. "They would ask us questions," Lúcia said, "then they would ask the same questions all over again. As soon as we saw a priest, if we could, we ran away. Every time we found ourselves before a priest, we prepared ourselves to offer to God one of our biggest sacrifices."

There were some exceptions among the priests. One was a source of great joy and encouragement to the children. "My dear girl," Lúcia remembers this priest saying to her, "you should love God a great deal for the favors and graces He is giving you." These words, said with such great kindness, engraved themselves so deeply on her heart, that since then she made it a habit to say continually to Our Lord, "My God, I love You, in gratitude for the graces You have given me."

Lúcia taught this prayer to her cousins. Jacinta loved it so much, that no matter what they were doing, she might interrupt everything to say to Lúcia, "Lúcia, have you forgotten to tell Our Lord that you love Him for the graces He has given us?"

There was another saintly old priest, a Father Cruz, a priest still venerated by all the people, who helped the children very much. One day, he went to Aljustrel and requested the children to take him to

54

the place where Our Lady appeared to them. Astride his donkey, flanked by the two girls, he rode over to the Cova da Iria, all the way teaching the girls new prayers. Jacinta remembered two of them, which she frequently said, and which gave her great consolation during her illness: "My God, I love You"; and "Sweet Heart of Mary, be my salvation." Explaining why she remembered these prayers, she said, "I want to tell Jesus that I love Him so much! When I say this to Him, it seems that I have a fire in my heart. I love Our Lord and Our Lady so much that I never get tired of telling Them that I love Them."

The Marto family was much more understanding of Jacinta and Francisco than was Lúcia's family of her. They questioned Lúcia and ridiculed her even more than outsiders. Her mother nagged her continually and went so far as to punish her. If we cannot excuse Senhora dos Santos, we can try to understand the mother's reasons for this course of action. They were a family of ordinary means. They had only a few head of cattle and a few pieces of land in the Cova da Iria where they raised their vegetables and food, potatoes, corn, beans and olives. Since the apparitions, so many people came to visit the Cova da Iria that the vegetables were trampled upon and everything was ruined. "My mother, lamenting her loss, would not spare me," Lúcia said. " 'When you want to eat, you can go now and ask that Lady!' and my sisters would say 'you should eat only what grows in the Cova da Iria.' "

This nagging became so distressing to the child, she hardly dared to pick up a slice of bread to eat. To make things worse, her older sisters who used to weave and sew to help support the home, now

55

had to help tend the sheep and they lost so much time with visitors, they could not do their work. Finally the family had to sell the sheep.

Lúcia's life at home grew more unbearable every day. Misunderstanding and misinterpretations multiplied with the hours. Her older sister, Maria dos Anjos, recalled, "One day, an old lady came to mother and told her that she was not surprised any more at the children saying that they had seen Our Lady. She had seen a lady give Lúcia half a dollar. Mother immediately called Lúcia and asked if that were true. Lúcia said that she had been given only two pennies. Mother persisted, using the old lady's words against Lúcia, 'Once a liar, always a liar,' and she used the broomstick on Lúcia. A few moments later Jacinta came in and showed us the half-dollar given her. But it was too late for Lúcia; she had already got her thrashing."

Some neighbors were as bad in their unbelief. They were very mean to the little ten-year-old girl, calling her evil names and, at times, even striking the child. No one dared to strike the Marto children, however; Ti Marto watched them too closely. Little Jacinta, in her eagerness to suffer for sinners, one day said to Lúcia, "I wish my parents were like yours so that they would hit me. Then I would have more sacrifices to offer to Our Lord."

Senhora Marto did act rather harshly at times but only at the first. "You are going to get it," she would say, "for your cheating the people. Many go to the Cova da Iria just because of you."

"But we don't force anyone to go there," Jacinta spoke up. "Whoever wants to go there goes. Whoever does not want to believe will be punished.

56

And mother, you look out, for if you don't believe . . ."

Meanwhile, Jacinta's father was being patient, mulling over the facts, trying to arrive at the truth. Like good Saint Joseph of old, Ti Marto was not going to judge hastily or do anything rash or unjust; he was thinking and praying, waiting for God to direct his course of thought and action.

Newspaper writers were not so considerate. The apparitions were reported in the papers, but the facts were placed in a wrong light, ridiculous details were invented and scorn was heaped upon this new "factory of miracles that the priests were setting up in Fátima." Trying to explain it away, the newspaper accounts accused the children and those who believed in them of being epileptics, the victims of fraud, greed or collective suggestions. The ridicule and accusations of the newspapers served but to divide the people, stirring up the enemies of the Church on the one hand, yet also serving to stir up the faith of the believers.

VII. *Fourth Apparition*

THE MAGISTRATE

THE VILLAGE OF FÁTIMA belongs to the County of Ourem. At the time of the apparitions the *Administrador* of the county, or Chief Magistrate, was Arthur Oliveira Santos, a man of tremendous political power. All administrative, political and sometimes even judicial power was centered in his hands.

Though he was a man of meagre education, a tin-smith by trade, he had been in politics since his youth. A baptised Catholic, he had abandoned the Church at the age of twenty to join the Masonic Lodge of Leiria. Later, he founded a lodge at Ourem of which he was the head. What added to his power was the fact that he published a local newspaper by which he endeavored to undermine the faith of the people in the Church and the priests.

When he heard about the apparitions of Fátima, he realized the effects they might have among the people. He realized, too, that if he allowed the Church to rise to new life in his county, he would be laughed to scorn by his friends and Masonic brethren. He counted on his immense power and the cringing spirit of the people to destroy this new religious fad in the beginning.

Although the citizenry of the county did cringe in fear before this all-powerful magistrate, there was one man who, when the good of his children and the good of the Church was threatened, had no fear. He would stand up boldly before any man in the interests of truth and justice. This man was Jacinta's father.

"My brother-in-law and I had both been summoned to appear at the County House, with Lúcia, at twelve noon, August the eleventh," Ti Marto reported. "Compadre Antonio and his daughter arrived at my house early in the morning before I had finished my breakfast. Lúcia's first question was, 'Aren't Jacinta and Francisco going too?' "

"Why should such little children go there?" Ti Marto replied. "No, I will answer for them."

Lúcia ran to Jacinta's room to inform her cousin of the summons they had received and how she feared she would be killed. "If they kill you, tell them that Francisco and I are like you and that we want to die too," Jacinta cried.

Lúcia and her father did not wait on Ti Marto, but went on ahead of him. Senhor Santos did not want to take a chance on being late and arousing the anger of the Magistrate. Lúcia rode the donkey, and as she rode along, she thought how different her father was from Ti Marto and her other uncles. "They put themselves in danger to defend their children but my parents turn me over with the greatest indifference so that they can do with me whatever they wish. But patience!" Lúcia comforted herself, "I expect to have to suffer more for Thy love, O my God, and it is for the conversion of sinners."

Ti Marto walked to the County House alone. When he reached the square in front of the house, he saw Lúcia and her father waiting there. "Has everything been settled already?" he inquired, thinking they had finished their audience with the Magistrate.

"No, the office was closed and no one was there." It was some while before they discovered that they had come to the wrong building. Finally they came before the Magistrate.

"Where is the boy?" He shouted right away at Ti Marto.

"What boy?" Ti Marto said. He continues to tell us what went on. "He did not know that there were three children involved, and as he had sent for only one, I pretended that I did not know what he meant. 'It's six miles from here to our village,' I told him, 'and the children can't walk that distance. They can't even stay on a donkey.' (Lúcia had fallen from the donkey three times in the journey.) I had

59

a mind to tell him some more things; imagine, the children so small wanted in court!

"He flared up and gave me a piece of his mind. What did I care! Then he began to question Lúcia, trying to pry the secret out of her. But she didn't say a word. Then he turned to her father, 'Do the people of Fátima believe in these things?' "

"Not at all. All that is just women's talk." Then the Magistrate turned towards me to see what I would say.

"I am here at your orders and I agree with my children!"

"You believe it is true?" he sneered at me.

"Yes, sir, I believe what they say." He laughed at me, but I didn't mind. The Magistrate then dismissed Lúcia, at the same time warning her that if he did not learn her secret, he would take her life."

The interview ended and they left for home.

Ti Marto thought he was through with the Magistrate. It wasn't as easy as that. The Magistrate had only begun the execution of his plans. It was almost time for the next apparition and this all-powerful official determined to prevent it at any cost.

"Monday morning, the thirteenth of August," Ti Marto recalled, "I had just begun hoeing my land when I was called home. As I entered the house I saw a group of strangers standing there, but that no longer surprised me. What did surprise me was finding my wife in the kitchen looking so worried. She didn't say a word, only motioned me to go to the front room. 'Why the hurry?' I said good and loud. But she kept waving me away. Still drying my hands, I went into the room, and who was there but the Magistrate! 'So you are here!' I said."

" 'Yes, of course, I want to see the miracle, too.'

"My heart warned me that something was wrong.

" 'Well, let's go,' he said, 'I'll take the children with me in my carriage. As Thomas said, "seeing is believing!" ' He was uneasy and glanced about nervously. 'Haven't the children come home yet? Time is passing. You had better call them!'

"They don't have to be called. They know when they are supposed to bring back the sheep and get ready." The children arrived almost at once and the Magistrate began urging them to go in his carriage. The children kept insisting it was not necessary.

" 'It's much better,' he repeated, 'for we'll get there faster and no one will bother us on the way.'

" 'Don't worry about that,' I said, 'they'll get there just the same.'

" 'You all go to Fátima,' he capitulated, 'and stop at the rectory because I want to ask the children a few questions.' As soon as we got to the rectory, he shouted to us from the balcony, 'Send up the first!'

" 'The first? Which one?' I snapped right back. I was upset by the premonition of some evil.

" 'Lúcia,' he said arrogantly.

" 'Go ahead, Lúcia,' I said to her," Ti Marto would remember this day well.

The Pastor was waiting in his office. He had changed his mind towards the apparitions. Now he considered them not the work of the devil, but plain inventions. He would call Lúcia to task, making sure that the Magistrate would realize he had no responsibility in these events. "Who taught you to say the things that you are going about saying?"

"The Lady whom I saw at the Cova da Iria."

"Anyone who goes around spreading such wicked lies as the lies you tell will be judged and will go to Hell if they are not true. More and more people are being deceived by you."

"If one who lies goes to Hell," answered the little girl, "then I will not go to Hell for I don't lie and tell only what I have seen and what the Lady has said to me. And as for the crowd that goes there, they go only because they want to. We don't call anyone."

"Is it true that the Lady has confided a secret to you?"

"Yes, but I can't tell it. But if Your Reverence wants to know it, I shall ask the Lady and if she gives me permission, I will tell you."

The Magistrate cut in as his plans would be spoiled if Lúcia was allowed to return to the Cova to ask permission to tell the Pastor the secret. "But those are supernatural matters," he said with finality.

"The whole thing was a hoax and sheer treachery on the Magistrate's part," Ti Marto continued. "When it came time for my children to go in, he said, 'That's enough. You may go; or better, let's all go for it's getting late.'

"The children started down the stairs. Meanwhile, the carriage was brought right up to the last step without my noticing it," Senhor Marto reported. "It was just perfect for him, for in a moment, he decoyed the children into it. Francisco sat in front and the two girls in the back. It was a cinch. The horse started trotting in the direction of the Cova da Iria. I relaxed. Upon reaching the road, the horse wheeled around, the whip cracking over him, and he bolted away like a flash. It was all so well planned and so well carried out. Nothing could be done now."

62

In the carriage, Lúcia spoke up first, though timidly, "This is not the way to the Cova da Iria." The Magistrate tried to make the children believe that he was taking them first to see the Pastor of the church at Ourem to consult with him. As they rode away, the people along the road realized that he was stealing the children and stoned him. Immediately, he covered them with a robe. When he reached his house, gloating over his success, he grabbed the children out of the carriage, pushed them inside and locked them in a room. "You won't leave this room until you tell me the secret," he warned them. They did not answer him a word.

"If they kill us, Jacinta consoled the other two when they were alone, "it doesn't matter. We'll go straight to Heaven."

Instead of an executioner with axe in hand the wife of the Magistrate came and proved herself very kind to the three little children. She took them from the room, gave them a good lunch and let them play with her children. She also gave them some picture books to look at.

THE "HOAX"

Meanwhile rumors had spread through the village that the devil would appear this time at the Cova da Iria to cause the earth to open up and swallow all those who were there. In spite of the rumor, however, many persons travelled to the holy spot. Maria de Capelinha was among them. She gives an eye-witness account of what went on.

"I was not afraid. I knew there was nothing evil about the apparitions because if there were, the people would not be praying at the Cova. My constant prayer as I walked along was, 'May Our Lady guide me according to God's Holy Will.' The crowd at the Cova on August thirteenth was even larger than in July.

"About eleven o'clock, Lúcia's sister, Maria dos Anjos, came with some candles to light to Our Lady. The people prayed and sang religious hymns around the holmoak. The absence of the children made them very restless. When it became known that the Magistrate had kidnapped them, a terrible resentment went through the crowd. There is no telling what it might have turned into, had it not thundered just then. Some thought the thunder came from the road; others thought that it came from the holmoak; but it seemed to me that it came from a distance. It frightened us all and many began to cry fearing they were going to be killed. Of course, no one was killed.

"Right after the thunder came a flash, and immediately, we all noticed a little cloud, very white, beautiful and bright, that came and stayed over the holmoak. It stayed a few minutes, then rose towards the heavens where it disappeared. Looking about, we noticed a strange sight that we had already seen and would see again. Everyone's face glowed, rose, red, blue, all the colors of the rainbow. The trees seemed to have no branches or leaves but were all covered with flowers; every leaf was a flower. The ground was in little squares, each one a different color. Our clothes seemed to be transformed also into the colors of the rainbow. The two vigil lanterns hanging from the arch over the holy spot appeared to be of gold.

"When the signs disappeared, the people seemed to realize that Our Lady had come and, not finding the children, had returned to Heaven. They felt that Our Lady was disappointed and hence they were exceedingly upset. Resentment grew in their hearts. They started towards the village, clamoring against the Magistrate, the Pastor and anyone they thought might have had anything to do with the arrest of the children."

Everything had been so beautiful but the sense of frustration at not having the children for the apparition made the people seethe with anger and roar out, "Let's go to Ourem to protest. Let's go and drench everything with blood. We'll get hold of the Pastor, for he is just as guilty . . . And the Regedor, we'll settle accounts with him."

Ti Marto, meanwhile, had gone to the Cova da Iria, and when this shouting of the people grew louder and louder, though he considered both the Pastor and the Magistrate guilty, he felt inspired to intervene in the tumult.

"Be calm, men, be calm." He shouted with all his might. "Don't hurt anyone. Whoever deserves punishment will get it. All this is by the power of the One above."

Indeed, the One above also intervened to preserve for His Mother the name of Fátima forever gracious and unstained, as is evidenced by the letter which the Pastor wrote the following day for the newspapers. It was published a few days later.

"The rumor that I was an accomplice to the sudden kidnapping of the children . . . I repel as an unjust and insidious calumny . . . The Magistrate did not confide the secret of his intentions to me . . .

"And if it was providential, for such it was, that the authority succeeded in taking the children away furtively and without resistance, no less providential was the calming of the spirits, excited by this devilish rumor. For otherwise the parish would have been mourning her Pastor today. Certainly, it was through the Virgin Mother that this snare of the devil did not strike him dead . . .

"The authority wanted the children to reveal a secret that they have told to no one . . . Thousands of witnesses say that the children were not necessary for the Queen of the Angels to manifest her power. They themselves will testify to the extraordinary occurrences which have now so deeply rooted their belief . . . The Virgin Mother does not need the presence of the pastor to show her kindness; and this itself should explain my absence and apparent indifference regarding a case so marvellous and sublime . . ."

THE ORDEAL

The children spent the night of the thirteenth in loneliness and prayer, beseeching Our Lady that they might have the strength to remain faithful to her always. When morning arrived, however, they were all taken to the County House where they were put through relentless questioning. The first to quiz them was an old lady, who used all her cunning and wiles to learn their secret. Later, the Magistrate tried bribes, offering them shiny gold coins; he made all kinds of promises to them and threatened them with every sort of punishment, but the children would not give in. This kept up all morning, broken only by lunch. They were put through the same inhuman "third degree" all afternoon. Finally, the Magistrate

66

told them he was going to put them in jail and have them thrown into a tank of boiling oil.

When they reached the jail, poor little Jacinta began to cry her eyes out. Lúcia and Francisco tried to comfort her.

"Why do you cry, Jacinta?" Lúcia said.

"Because we are going to die without ever again seeing our parents. None of them have come to see us, neither yours nor mine. They don't care for us anymore. I want to see my mother, at least."

"Don't cry, Jacinta," Francisco interrupted, "we are offering this sacrifice for sinners." Then the three raised their hands towards Heaven, repeating together, "My Jesus, all this is for love of You and for sinners."

"And for the Holy Father," Jacinta put in, not wishing to forget any request of Our Lady, "and in reparation for the offenses against the Immaculate Heart of Mary."

There were many men imprisoned in the jail at that same time, and not one of them, no matter how hard a criminal he might have been, could remain unmoved at the sight of the three little children. Each of the men took his turn trying to console the children or to shake them from their purpose of retaining the secret.

"Why don't you tell it to him?"

"Why should you care?"

"Never," Jacinta said, " we would rather die."

The children did not seem to mind in the least their being imprisoned in jail. But seven year old Jacinta could not accustom herself to the thought of dying without first seeing her mother. To distract her, the prisoners began singing, playing the accordion and dancing. They tried to get the children to

67

dance with them, and one very tall man picked up Jacinta in his arms and danced around with her. The thought of Our Lady flashed through her mind; dancing was not the right preparation for Heaven. So Jacinta made the man stop; she took the medal from around her neck, asked the man to hang it from a nail on the wall, then she knelt with Francisco and Lúcia to say the Rosary. Embarrassed and ashamed, the prisoners also got on their knees. One man still kept his hat on. Francisco got up, went over to him and said, "When we pray, we take our hats off." The man took it off and dropped it on the floor. Francisco picked it up and laid it on the bench.

Soon, they heard steps outside. A guard entered, looking at the children, he barked, "Come with me."

Again they were taken to the County House and put through the third degree. Jacinta was called in first, "The oil is already boiling. Tell the secret . . . otherwise . . ." Jacinta, like Our Lord before the judges, remained silent.

"Take her away and throw her into the tank!" yelled the inquisitor. The guard grabbed her arm, swung her around and locked her in another room.

Outside the Magistrate's office, while awaiting their turn, Francisco confided to Lúcia, "If they kill us, we shall soon be in Heaven. Nothing else counts. I hope that Jacinta does not get scared. I should say a *Hail Mary* for her." He took off his cap and said a prayer.

The guard, watching the children, was puzzled at the boy's behavior. "What are you saying?" he demanded.

"I am saying one *Hail Mary* for Jacinta, to give her courage."

68

The other guard came back, and led Francisco into the Magistrate's office. Grabbing hold of the boy, he shouted, "Spit out the secret. The other one is already burned up; now it's your turn. Go ahead, out with it."

"I can't!" he replied, looking calmly into the eyes of this new Nero. "I can't tell it to anyone."

"You say you can't. That's your business. Take him away. He'll share his sister's lot." The boy was taken into the next room, where he found Jacinta, safe and happy.

Lúcia was convinced that they had been killed and thinking that she was next to be thrown into the burning cauldron of oil, she trusted in her Heavenly Mother not to desert her, but to give her the courage to be loyal and courageous even as Francisco and Jacinta were.

Though Lúcia did tell the Magistrate something of what happened in the visions, even as she had told her parents and the Pastor, she kept the secret part to herself. It was a solemn promise to Our Lady and she would rather die than break it. The Magistrate was not satisfied with this little bit. He wanted to know the secret. After her inquisition, Lúcia too was locked in the room where the other two were and how happy they were for their unwavering fidelity to Our Lady.

The Magistrate did not yet give up. The guard came in to remind them that soon they would be thrown into the burning oil. The thought of being able to die together for Our Lady made them all the happier. The Magistrate finally admitted, after further fruitless questioning, that he could accomplish nothing. Then out of fear of what the enraged people might do, he himself took them in his carriage to Fatima, hardly realizing that the Church was celebrating on that day the Feast of the Assumption.

THE SECRET

When the people filed out of Church, after attending Mass on the Holy Day, they congregated in the yard. The one topic on all lips was what had happened to the children. As Ti Marto came out, they all asked, "Where are the children?"

"How do I know," he replied, "Maybe they took them to Santarem, the capital. The day they kidnaped them, my stepson, Antonio, went with some other boys to Ourem, and he saw the children playing on the veranda of the Magistrate's house. That's the last news I heard."

He had hardly said these words, when someone shouted, "Look, Ti Marto, Look! The children are on the rectory balcony!"

Ti Marto recalls his feelings. "I can't say how quickly I got there and swept Jacinta in my arms. I couldn't say a word. Tears ran down my face, wetting the child's face. Francisco and Lúcia both threw their arms around me, saying, 'Father, your blessing! Uncle, your blessing!' (as the custom is in Portugal, when children return home after an absence).

"A public official and underling of the Magistrate approached me. He shook from head to foot. I never saw the like before. 'Here you have the children!' he said. I wanted to speak my mind but I restrained myself and remarked, 'This might have come to a sorry end. They wanted the children to contradict

70

themselves, but they failed. Even if they succeeded, I would always say they spoke the truth.' "

The people in the church-yard were in an uproar, shaking their fists, swinging their staffs. Everyone was restless. The Pastor left the Church immediately, and started up the stairs into the rectory. Suspecting that Ti Marto was stirring up the people against him, he said in rebuke, "Senhor Manuel, you scandalize me."

"I knew how to answer him then," recalls Ti Marto, and the Pastor went into the house. Ti Marto could not at the time realize the noble role the Pastor was playing that day. Ti Marto then turned to the crowd in the yard and, still holding his little Jacinta in his arms, he shouted, "Boys, behave yourselves! Some of you are shouting against the Senhor Prior, others against the Administrador, and still some against the Regedor. No one is to blame. The blame lies with the lack of faith and all has been allowed by the One above."

The Pastor heard this and was very pleased, so he said from the window, "Senhor Manuel speaks very well; he speaks very well."

The Magistrate had gone to the inn, and when he returned, seeing the crowd and Ti Marto in the balcony of the rectory, he shouted at him, "Stop that, Senhor Marto!"

"All right; all right. There is nothing wrong." The Magistrate then went into the Pastor's office and called Ti Marto in.

The rage of the people had subsided. The generous Pastor was allowing the people to believe that he had shared in the abduction of the children in order to save the Magistrate. The prudent words of a man of faith had the power to keep the crowd

71

below under control. It was a fine proof of the power of religion, and the Pastor did not miss his chance to point out the fact to the Magistrate. "You must realize, Senhor Administrador, that religion is a necessity also."

As Ti Marto was leaving, the Magistrate turned to him, saying, "Senhor Marto, come and have a glass of wine with me."

"Don't bother now, thanks." However, he noticed a group of young men on the street, armed with staffs. It made him fear that they might clash with the Magistrate. It was better that everything end in peace, so he stood at the Magistrate's side, thinking within himself that it might be the wise thing to accept his invitation.

"I am grateful," the Magistrate said, realizing what he was doing. He felt safe. "You ask the children if I did not treat them right."

"All right. All right . . . There's no hard feelings. The people think more of asking questions than I do." Just then the children came down the stairs, and headed for the Cova da Iria without losing a moment. The people began to go home and the Magistrate and Ti Marto went to an inn.

Of their conversation over the wine Ti Marto later recalled, "The whole thing bored me very much, for he was trying to convince me that the children had told him the secret. 'Very well, very well,' I said, 'They did not tell it to their father or mother, but they did tell it to you!' "

With that the matter ended for the time being. It is important to note, however, that the interrogation of the children served one purpose that was providential. Since everything became a matter of

72

official record, the Magistrate unwittingly made the existence of a secret revelation undeniable.

THE NINETEENTH OF AUGUST

On the following Sunday, the 19th of August, the children, according to their custom, went to the Cova da Iria after Mass. There they said the Rosary, then returned to Aljustrel. After lunch, Lúcia, together with Francisco and his elder brother John, left for a place called Valinhos, not far away, where they intended to spend the afternoon.

The afternoon passed quickly, but towards four o'clock, Lúcia became aware of the signs that always immediately preceded the apparitions of Our Lady: the sudden cooling of the air, the paling of the sun, and the typical flash. The children had already been having a wonderful premonition that they were to experience the supernatural again. Now Our Lady was about to come and Jacinta was not there! Lúcia called out to John, "Go quickly and get Jacinta, Our Lady is coming!"

The boy did not want to go. He too wanted to see Our Lady. "Go fast," Lúcia insisted, "and I will give you four pennies, if you bring Jacinta back with you. Here's two now and I'll keep the other two for you when you return."

John took the pennies and started running home. When he reached his house, he called in, "Mother, mother, Lúcia wants Jacinta!"

"Aren't the three of you enough for your games? Can't you leave her alone for a minute?" the mother answered back.

"Let her come, little mother, they want her there

73

now. See, Lúcia gave me two pennies to make sure I would bring her."

Two pennies! That was a lot of money for little children to give away so easily. "What does she want Jacinta for now?"

John, wriggling like an eel, burst out, "Because Lúcia has already seen the signs in the skies and she wants Jacinta there in a hurry."

"God be with you; Jacinta is at her godmother's house."

John bolted off to get her. There, he whispered the news to Jacinta, and together, hand in hand, they raced over to Valinhos so as not to miss Our Lady. Just as John and Jacinta reached the field, a second flash rent the air. A few moments later, the brilliant Lady appeared over a holmoak, a slightly taller one than that at the Cova da Iria. The Lady was rewarding the children for their fidelity.

"What do you want of me?" Lúcia asked.

"I want you to continue to come to the Cova da Iria on the thirteenth and to continue to say the Rosary every day."

Lúcia then told Our Lady of her anguish at the unbelief of so many in the reality of her presence. She asked Our Lady if she would be willing to perform a miracle that all might see and believe.

"Yes," Our Lady answered, *"In the last month, in October, I shall perform a miracle so that all may believe in my apparitions. If they had not taken you to the village, the miracle would have been greater. Saint Joseph will come with the Baby Jesus to give peace to the world. Our Lord also will come to bless the people. Besides, Our Lady of the Rosary and Our Lady of Sorrows will come."*

Lúcia remembered Senhora da Capelinha's request

74

and said: "What do you wish us to do with the money and the offerings that the people leave at the Cova da Iria?"

"Two litters should be made; you and Jacinta are to carry one with two other girls dressed in white; Francisco is to carry the other with three boys also dressed in white robes. The money placed on the litters is for the Feast of Our Lady of the Rosary."

Lúcia then spoke to Our Lady of the sick who had been recommended to her.

"Yes, I shall cure some of them within the year." But she went on teaching them to pray rather for the health of souls than of bodies, *"Pray! Pray a great deal and make sacrifices for sinners, for many souls go to Hell for not having someone to pray and make sacrifices for them."*

The Lady took leave of her little friends and began to rise towards the East, as before. John was disappointed. He tried hard to see Our Lady but had seen nothing. However, he heard something like the hissing of a rocket, when Lúcia said, "Jacinta, see Our Lady is going away." It gave John small consolation.

The three children who had stood by helplessly at the Cova da Iria when the older people stripped the holmoak of its foliage, broke off the small branch which the resplendent robe of Our Lady had touched. John and Lúcia stayed at the Valinhos with the sheep while Francisco and Jacinta rushed home with the precious branch to tell their parents of the unexpected visit of Our Lady.

As they passed Lúcia's house, her mother and sister were at the door with some neighbors. "Aunt Maria Rosa," Jacinta cried out with joy, "We saw Our Lady again! It was at the Valinhos!"

75

"My, what little liars you turned out to be! As if Our Lady would appear to you wherever you go!"

"But we did see her," Jacinta insisted. "See here, Our Lady had one foot on this twig and the other on that one."

"Give it to me. Let me see." Jacinta gave the branch to Lúcia's mother. The mother's face showed great surprise as she put the branch to her nose. "What does this smell of?" she said, continuing to smell it. "It is not perfume, it's not incense nor perfumed soap; it's not the smell of roses nor anything I know but it is a good smell." The whole family gathered and each wanted to hold the branch and smell the beautiful odor. "Leave it here, Jacinta. Someone will come along who will be able to tell what kind of an odor it is."

From that moment, Lúcia's mother and her whole family began to modify their opposition towards the apparitions. Jacinta then took the branch and hurried home to show it to her own mother and father. Ti Marto tells of the occasion in his own words.

"I had taken a round of my properties on that day. After sunset, as I was drawing near my house, a friend of mine met me and said, 'Ti Marto, the miracle is becoming clearer.'

"'What do you mean?' I said, not knowing anything about the apparition at Valinhos or the branch.

"'You know, Our Lady appeared again, just a little while ago, to your children and Lúcia at Valinhos. You can believe it is true. I want to tell you that your Jacinta has something special. She had not gone with the others and a boy came to call her. Our Lady did not appear until she arrived!' I shrugged my shoulders. I didn't know what to answer, but I was thinking about what my friend said as I reached the yard of my house. My wife was not at home. I went into the kitchen and sat down. Jacinta came right in with a big smile on her face and a little branch in her hand.

" 'Look, father, Our Lady appeared to us again at the Valinhos!'

"As she came in, I sensed a magnificent fragrance which I could not explain. I stretched out my hands towards the branch saying, 'What are you bringing in, Jacinta?'

" 'It is the little branch on which Our Lady placed her feet.' I smelled it but the odor had gone." Our Lady did not have to perform a miracle to prove her case to him.[6]

VIII. *Fifth Apparition*

THE WORDS that most deeply embedded themselves on the minds of the children were the last words spoken by Our Lady at Valinhos, "Pray, pray a great deal, and make sacrifices for sinners, for many souls go to Hell for not having someone to pray and make sacrifices for them." These words awakened in the children an even stronger desire for mortification, prayer and suffering. Their one longing was to close that terrifying furnace of Hell so that no more souls could go there.

[6] When Lúcia's sister, Teresa, and her husband were coming into the village of Fátima, they noticed the cooling of the air, the paling of the sun and the pattern of different colors over everything, the same as happened at the Cova da Iria six days previous, when the children were prevented from going to the Cova because of their arrest and imprisonment. This was the very hour of the apparition at Valinhos.

When alone in the fields with their sheep, the three youngsters spent hour after hour in the gully of the Cabeço where the Angel had appeared, prostrate upon the ground, repeating the prayer the Angel had taught them. "My God, I believe, I adore, I hope, and I love You. I beg pardon of You for those who do not believe, do not adore, do not hope, and do not love You . . . Most Holy Trinity, Father, Son and Holy Ghost, I adore You profoundly and I offer You the most Precious Body, Blood, Soul and Divinity of Jesus Christ, present in all the tabernacles of the world, in reparation for the outrages, sacrileges, and indifferences by which He Himself is offended. And by the infinite merits of His Most Sacred Heart and the Immaculate Heart of Mary, I beg of You the conversion of poor sinners."

When this cramped position became unbearable, they changed positions and said the Rosary, adding the special prayer Our Lady had taught them, "O My Jesus, forgive us; save us from the fire of Hell; bring all souls to Heaven; especially those in most need."

The children prayed much, but they sacrificed themselves even more. They strained their minds to discover new ways of suffering for the conversion of sinners. Lest others misunderstand the motives of their mortifications and prevent them from saving souls from Hell, they kept this a secret between themselves and Our Lady. Only under orders from her superiors many years later, did Lúcia relate the extent of their youthful prayers and sacrifices.

Watching the sheep on the hot barrenness of the hills, they offered up to God and Our Lady their burning thirst. The children went for days without

78

drinking anything while they were alone in the fields. This was one of their biggest and most difficult sacrifices. Indeed, that summer they went the whole month of August without water. Lúcia tells how one day, as the three of them walked by the pond of Carreira on their way home from Cova da Iria, Jacinta was so overcome with thirst, she was forced to speak out, "Look, I am so thirsty, my head aches so much. I'm going to drink a little of this water."

"Not that water," Lúcia said. "My mother doesn't want us to touch that water. People do their washing in it and the animals drink it. It will make us sick. We'll go over and ask Aunt Maria dos Anjos to give us a little water."

"No, Lúcia," Jacinta spoke up, "I don't want good water. I'll drink this since I can offer to Our Lord the sacrifice of drinking of this foul water instead of my thirst."

Another day, the children were playing, as their mothers thought, by the well, when Jacinta's mother brought them a few bunches of grapes to munch on. As soon as her mother went away, Jacinta said, "Let's not eat them. We'll offer this sacrifice." Just then, she saw some poor children on the road, so she ran over to give them the luscious looking grapes. On another occasion, Senhora Olimpia gave Jacinta a basket of figs for the three of them. They sat on the ground and started to eat them when Jacinta remembered the sinners whom she wanted so much to save from the fire of Hell. She put hers back and ran off for a while so that she would not give in to the desire for the figs. While they were picking some little plants that grow between rocks and burst with a crack when squeezed, Jacinta hurt herself in some nettles. One would think she found a big diamond. "Look," she exclaimed, "I found something else for our mortifications."

Another day, while pasturing their sheep, they found a piece of rope. Playfully, Lúcia tied it around her arm and soon discovered that it hurt. "Look, this hurts! We could tie this around our body for another sacrifice." The rope was thick and very rough. They cut it in three pieces and tied it around their waists. The sharp pain it caused was difficult to endure, especially for little Jacinta. Lúcia suggested that she take it off, but Jacinta insisted she keep it on. She would willingly endure any sacrifice to save sinners from Hell. They even wore the rope to bed. This prevented them from getting the rest they needed and Our Lady spoke about it in her next visit.

While the children sought every means of pleasing Our Lady, there were men determined to discredit the children and make a fiasco of the apparitions. For them, it was another opportunity to destroy the Church in Portugal. When the local magistrate found his efforts foiled, another man arose to take up the cudgel. He was José do Vale, the editor of a leftist newspaper. His idea was to put an end to the Fátima affair by having a public meeting and distributing pamphlets in the towns and villages telling the "truth" about Fátima and the Church. José do Vale thought that the best time to get the people together would be after the last Mass at the Church of Fátima.

Anticipating easy success, he went there on a Sunday morning with some guards and a few influential people of the district. The only man in the church-yard was the *Regedor,* the village Magistrate.

The place of Mass had been unexpectedly and quietly changed this Sunday by the Pastor, who occasionally alternated between the several churches in the parish.

Not to be outdone, the group proceeded to the Cova da Iria where they knew would be many people. An unusual reception awaited them. A man had mustered some donkeys, which he had tied to the holmoaks. As soon as the men appeared, he tricked the donkeys into braying and kept them at it, to the very great annoyance of the unwelcome visitors.

José do Vale went towards the holmoak where another surprise awaited the group. There was a pile of straw and feed placed around the tree. The good people of Moita invited them to eat it, likening them to the animals that live on such things. "It was an insult and they took it as such," Maria da Capelinha said. "I got there about half past eleven with two of my neighbors. We hid ourselves so that we could be close to the men when they came. The Chapel of the Confessions is now on the spot where we hid. Further up, three men sat on the branches of a large holmoak. One of the evil men started to talk against the Church and every time he said something especially wicked, we answered, '*Viva Jesús e Maria;* Hail Jesus and Mary!' A boy standing on another large holmoak opposite us echoed loud after us, 'Hail Jesus, Hail Mary,' taking off his hat each time in great reverence.

"The men became so disgusted that they sent two guards after us, but we cut across the fields and they lost sight of us. Meanwhile, Mass was over and our menfolk came along. When they realized what was going on, they began to heckle the speakers and make fun of the guards. 'Mule-heads, mule-heads, mule-heads.' José and his cohorts started calling the men 'mountain clodhoppers' and 'hillbillies', etc. They sent the guards after them but the men scampered to the right and left, laughing and poking fun at the men who were going to reveal the 'whole truth' about the Church and Our Lady. José do Vale and his crowd were never heard from again."

Meantime the three children counted the hours to the next apparition. Many thousands believed and as many still refused to believe in the apparitions. This unbelief and misunderstanding, especially on the part of the priests, together with the constant, repetitious questions of the people caused the children keen suffering and a sense of utter loneliness. They felt that no one but Our Lady really understood them and that only they understood her.

The thirteenth of September was at hand. As the day broke, crowds stormed the homes of the children and everyone wanted to speak to them to ask a special remembrance to Our Lady. "When it came time to leave for the Cova da Iria," Lúcia wrote, "I left with Jacinta and Francisco, but there were so many people that we could hardly move a step. The roads overflowed with people. Everyone wanted to see and speak to us. There was no human respect in that crowd. Ordinary people, even noble ladies and gentlemen, succeeding in breaking their way through the crowd surrounding us, fell on their knees before us, asking that we bring their needs before Our Lady. Many others, unable to get near us, shouted, 'for the love of God, ask Our Lady to cure my lame child . . . ask her to make my child see . . . to make my child hear . . . ask her to bring my husband and son back from the war . . .

82

to convert a sinner . . . to make me, sick with tuberculosis, whole again.' There could be seen all .he miseries and afflictions of mankind. Some shouted even from the trees and walls which they had climbed in order to see us.

"To some we said, 'Yes.' To others we lent a hand to help them rise from the dust on the ground. Thanks to a few gentlemen who opened a way for us through the crowds, we were able to move along. When I read now in the New Testament of the enchanting scenes that accompanied the passage of Our Lord through Palestine, I remember these others, that Our Lady made me, who was so young, witness on the roads and lanes from Aljustrel to Fátima and the Cova da Iria. I thank Our Lord as I offer him the faith of our good Portuguese people; and I think that if these people humbled themselves so much before three poor children, only because there was given to them, in all mercy, the grace of speaking with the Mother of God, what would they not have done if they were to see Jesus Christ Himself?"

When they finally arrived at the holmoak, Lúcia as usual started the Rosary, with the people responding. They were almost finished when the children arose to scan the horizon. They had seen the flash. Our Lady would soon come. A few moments passed. A globe of light appeared before the crowd, and the all holy Queen of Angels was standing over the holmoak.

"What do you want of me?" Lúcia spoke very humbly.

"Let the people continue to say the Rosary every day to obtain the end of the war," Our Lady responded, at the same time renewing the promises

83

she made during her last apparition. *"In the last month, in October, I shall perform a miracle so that all may believe in my apparitions. If they had not taken you to the village, the miracle would have been greater. Saint Joseph will come with the Baby Jesus to give peace to the world. Our Lord also will come to bless the people. Besides Our Lady of the Rosary and Our Lady of Sorrows will come.*

"God is pleased with your sacrifices but does not wish that you sleep with the rope. Wear it only during the day."

"They have requested me to ask you many things," Lúcia then said. "This girl is a deaf mute. Don't you want to cure her?"

"In the course of the year she will be improved."

"Will you help these other people?"

"Some I will cure: but the others, no. Our Lord does not have confidence in them."

"The people would like very much to have a chapel built here," Lúcia suggested.

"Use half of the money received so far for the litters. On one of them, place the statue of Our Lady of the Rosary. The other half should be set aside to help with the building of the chapel."

"Many people say that I am a swindler who should be hanged or burned. Please perform a miracle for all to believe."

"Yes, in October, I will perform a miracle so that all may believe."

"Some people gave me these two letters for you and a bottle of cologne." Lúcia did not want to forget any requests.

"None of that is necessary for Heaven."

Our Lady then began to leave. Lúcia, pointing towards the East, shouted to the people, "If you want

84

to see Our Lady, look that way!" They looked eagerly towards the East and many saw the luminous globe now ascending towards Heaven. As soon as it disappeared, the whole crowd swarmed upon the children asking them a thousand questions . . . "What did Our Lady say? . . . Will she cure my boy? . . . Will my husband come home from the war safe? . . . Will she help my little girl?" It was with great difficulty that the parents reclaimed their children and brought them home. When they reached home, hundreds more waited to ask the children more questions. "What did Our Lady look like? . . . Was it really Our Lady? . . . Tell us everything that happened."

Among the many witnesses of this apparition, there were a few priests, including the Vicar General of Leiria, Monsignor John Quaresma and Father Manuel do Carmo Gois. The Monsignor, a man of great learning, came to the Cova da Iria with many questions in his mind; he didn't know whether to believe or not in the testimony of the children. He gives us his own personal account of the happenings of this day.

He had been thinking, ". . . have the little shepherds been the victims of a beautiful mirage? . . ." Was there any truth in the words of the children? . . . What should we say of the evergrowing multitudes that on every thirteenth asserted that they saw extraordinary signs in the skies of Fátima?

"I left, the morning of September the thirteenth, 1917, in a slow carriage drawn by an old horse, to go to the place of the apparitions. Father Gois chose a spot overlooking the vast amphitheater of the Cova da Iria. From it we could easily see, without coming too close, the place where the little shepherds prayed as they waited for the heavenly apparition. At noontime, silence fell on the crowd, and a low whispering of prayers could be heard. Suddenly, cries of joy rent the air, many voices praising the Blessed Virgin. Arms were raised to point to something above, 'Look! don't you see?' . . . 'Yes, I see it!'

"I, too, raised my eyes to probe the amplitude of the skies, hoping to see what the other more fortunate eyes were seeing before me. There was not a single cloud in the whole blue sky, yet to my great astonishment, I saw clearly and distinctly a luminous globe, coming from the east to the west, gliding slowly and majestically through space. My friend also looked up, and had the happiness of enjoying the same unexpected but enchanting apparition. Suddenly, the globe with its extraordinary light, disappeared before our eyes.

"There was a little girl near us, dressed like Lúcia and about the same age. She was excited with joy and kept saying, 'I still see her . . . now she is coming down.' A few minutes later the child exclaimed again, pointing to the skies, 'Now she is rising again,' following the globe with her eyes until it disappeared towards the sun.

"I asked my friend, who was enthusiastic over what we had seen, 'What do you think of that globe?' Without any hesitation, he replied, 'That was Our Lady.' That was also my belief. The three little shepherds had seen the Mother of God herself; to us had been given the grace to see the chariot that had borne her from Heaven to the barren inhospitable hills of Aire. It must be said that everyone around us had seen the same as we. For on all sides were heard manifestations of joy, and greetings to

86

Our Lady. Some, however, saw nothing; for one good and pious soul nearby wept bitterly for not having seen.

"My colleague went about from group to group in the Cova da Iria, and afterwards along the road, to inquire of each what they had seen. The persons interrogated were of the most various classes; yet with one voice they affirmed the reality of the phenomena which we ourselves had contemplated.

"Deeply satisfied, we returned home from our pilgrimage to Fátima, with the firm purpose of coming back on the thirteenth of October to accede to Lúcia's invitation and to fortify even more our faith in the apparitions of Our Lady."

Other signs were reported on this day. There was a sudden cooling of the air; and the sun was dimmed, so much so that thousands of people could see the stars even though it was mid-day. Also there was a rain of irridescent petals that vanished upon reaching the ground.

IX. *Sixth Apparition*

DURING THE LAST THREE APPARITIONS, Our Lady promised the children that the last time she would appear, in October, she would effect a miracle that everyone would see and thereby believe. Lúcia had repeated this promise to others and the news of it had spread like wild-fire throughout the whole country. Think of it, being warned ahead of time that a very great miracle would happen not a hundred years from now but within the next thirty days. The expectation, the anxiety of waiting for this tremendous sign weighed heavily on believers, especially on the children's families. Unbelievers sneered at the prediction and the enemies of the Church called it a huge hoax that the Church was trying to put over on the people. For them, October the thirteenth would be a day of great celebration, the day when the hoax would be revealed and the Church completely discredited.

The children were greatly saddened at the unbelief of so many, but they had full trust in the goodness of Our Lady; so they had no worries. Their families, however, were tormented, especially by the neighbors, so many of whom would not believe in the apparitions. They even threatened the family with severe penalties if this promise turned out to be a hoax.

"My family was extremely worried," Maria dos Anjos, Lúcia's oldest sister, stated. "The closer the day came, the more we insisted with Lúcia that she give up this dream of hers. We would all have to suffer because of her imaginings. Father scolded her often, though he never struck her. Mother was not so easy. One rumor was going around that they would place bombs at the Cova da Iria to scare everyone that went there. Some people suggested that mother lock the children in a room until they denied the whole story. We did not speak of it in front of Lúcia, but we were frightened and we wondered what was going to happen to us. Some others suggested we take Lúcia away some place where no one could find her. We didn't know what to do.

"Mother wanted to do what was right but she didn't understand. 'If it were Our Lady,' mother lamented, 'she could have performed a miracle already, start a spring or something else. Oh, how will all this end.' But the children showed no fear at all. I went to the children one day as they were speaking together at the well. 'Have you decided yet that you saw nothing? They are warning us that they will throw bombs at our homes,' I said. 'Tell it only to me and I'll tell the Pastor. Do you want me to tell him? Do you?' Lúcia frowned but did not speak. Jacinta, with tears in her eyes, said very softly, 'Yes, you may do as you wish, but we have seen!' "

Lúcia's mother was so panic-stricken by the thought of impending disaster that on the morning of the twelfth, she jumped out of bed, ran into Lúcia's room and begged her to go to Confession. "People say we're going to die tomorrow; they'll kill us if the miracle doesn't happen."

"If you want to go to Confession, mother, I'll go with you," she answered very calmly, "but I'm not afraid. I am positive that the Lady will do what she promised to do tomorrow." After this, nothing more was said about confession.

Things were different in the Marto home. Nothing could shake the belief of Senhor Marto. He tells how the Pastor of Porto de Mós came with one of his parishioners, a few days before the thirteenth. He wanted to make the children contradict themselves. He questioned Francisco and got nowhere. He wanted to talk to Lúcia and Jacinta but they had gone with a donkey to Boleiros to bring home some lime. The priest wouldn't wait for them to return, but went after them with the older boy, John. He was going to force the children to deny their story, or else. . . .

"Listen, good girl," the priest said to Lúcia, "you are going to tell me that it is all an invention. Even if you don't admit it, I'll say it is and I'll have it spread everywhere, and you won't escape either."

Lúcia did not say a word, but Senhor Marto spoke up, "The best thing to do is to telegraph everywhere immediately."

"Exactly what we should do! No one will come here on the thirteenth," the priest said triumphantly.

The man with him said, "This is nothing but witchcraft."

Senhor Marto became very angry at this, so Jacinta vanished because she abhorred any display of anger. Then her father said to the priest, "If you're going to do that, leave the children alone. No one will stop you from doing what you please." Senhor Marto took the children home, followed by the priest and his companion. They saw Jacinta sitting on the porch combing another little girl's hair.

"Listen, Jacinta," said the priest, "so you did not want to tell us anything. Lúcia has told the whole story. It's a lie."

"No, Lúcia told nothing," she answered very firmly. He kept insisting but Jacinta was just as insistent. They were baffled by the firmness of the child, so much so that Senhor Marto thought they would come to believe in the apparitions. Then the man took a dime out of his pocket to give to Jacinta.

Senhor Marto reached out his hand to stop the man, "Stop. That should never be done!" he said.

"Can't I at least give John something?"

"It is not necessary," the father answered, "but if you wish, you may."

As they were going, the priest turned to Senhor Marto and said, "You have played your role well."

"Well or not, I don't know. But here in my house, this is the way we do things. You did not succeed in making the children contradict themselves. Even if you did, I would have stuck to my belief that they have been speaking the truth." Senhor Marto was a good father, loyal always to his children even as they were loyal to him, because they all believed implicitly in God and His Holy Mother Mary.

On the morning of October 13, 1917, fear and panic prevailed in Fátima. Rain was pouring from the heavens, a sad beginning for the glorious day promised by Our Lady and the children. The rain, however, did not dampen the spirits of the many thousands of people who came from every section of Portugal to witness the miracle promised. Even the daily newspapers, until now so inimical to the happenings at Fátima, sent reporters to the scene, and since for days afterwards they carried long articles on the unusual events, we will use excerpts from the newspaper accounts to give an authentic history of the occasion.

"Nearby communities, towns and villages, emptied of people," said the reporter for "O Dia," a Lisbon newspaper. "For days prior to the thirteenth, groups of pilgrims travelled towards Fátima. They came on foot, buskins on their brawny legs, food bags on their heads, across the pine groves, where the crowberries seem like drops of dew upon the verdure, along the sands, where the windmills rotate. A slow and swaying gait swung the hems of their skirts from side to side and waved orange kerchiefs upon which sat their black hats.

"Workers from Marinha, farmers from Monte Real, Cortes and Marrazes, women from distant hills, the hills of Soubio, Minde and Louriçal, people from everywhere whom the voice of the miracle had reached, left their homes and fields and came

91

on foot, by horse or by carriage. They travelled the highways and the roads, between hills and pine groves. For two days these came to life with the rolling of the carriages, the trot of the donkeys and the voices of the pilgrims.

"Fall gave tints of red to the vineyards. A chilly and piercing northeaster, forerunner of winter, waved the transparent poplars along the margins of the rivers.

"Over the sands, the white sails of the windmills rotated. In the woods, the green tops of the pines bowed to the wind. Clouds slowly closed the skies, while the fog rolled in with light, soft puffs. In the vast beach of Vieira, the sea foamed, roared and coiled in high waves, as the sinister howl of its voice travelled over the fields.

"All night long and into early morning, a light persistent rain fell. It soaked the fields, saddened the air, and chilled to the bone the men, women and children and the beasts plodding their way towards the hill of the miracle. The rain kept falling, a soft, unending drizzle. Drops trickled down the women's skirts of coarse wool or striped cotton, making them as weighty as lead. Water dripped from the caps and broad-brimmed hats onto the new jackets of their suits for seeing God. The bare feet of the women and the hobnailed shoes of the men sloshed in the wide pools of the muddy roads. They seemed not to notice the rain. They went up the hills without stopping, illuminated by faith, anxious for the miracle promised by Our Lady to the pure and simple children who watched sheep, for the thirteenth at one o'clock, the hour of the sun.

"A murmur drifting down from the hills reached us. It was a murmur like the distant voice of the sea lowered to a faint before the silence of the fields. It was the religious songs, now becoming clear, intoned by thousands of voices. On the plateau, over a hill, or filling a valley, there was a wide and shuffling mass of thousands upon thousands of souls in prayer."

"*O Seculo*," another Lisbon newspaper, carried an extensive article on the occurrences of the day. Their reporter chose for his observation point the road between Chão de Maçãs and Ourem.

"Along the road, we met the first groups going to the holy place, many walking more than ten miles, men and women, most of them barefoot, with the women carrying bags on their heads, topped with their heavy shoes, while the men leaned on their sturdy staffs and carried their umbrellas as a precaution. They seemed unaware of all that happened around them, disinterested in either the landscape or the other wayfarers, saying the Rosary in a sad rhythm, as if immersed in a dream. A woman broke out with the first part of the *Hail Mary*, the hailing; her companions took up in chorus the second part, the supplication. With slow cadenced steps, they threaded along the dusty road, among pine groves and olive orchards, so that they might arrive before nightfall at the place of the apparition. There in the open, under the cold light of the stars, they planned to sleep and get the best places near the blessed holmoak to enable them to have a better view.

"As they entered the town, some women, already infected by the environment with the virus of atheism, joked about the great event. 'Aren't you going tomorrow to see the saint?' one asked. 'Me? No! Not unless she comes to see me!' They laughed heartily but the devout went on indifferent to anything which was not the motive of their pilgrimage. All night long, the most varied vehicles moved into the town square carrying the faithful and the curious, and also old ladies, somberly dressed, weighted by the years. The ardent fire of faith shining in their eyes gave them heart to leave for a day the little corner in the home from which they were inseparable.

"At dawn, new groups surged undauntedly and crossed through the villages, without stopping for a moment, breaking the early morning silence with their beautiful religious hymns. The delicate harmony of the women's voices made violent contrast with their rustic appearance.

"The sun was rising, though the skies presaged a storm. Dark clouds loomed directly over Fátima. Nothing would stop the crowd converging from every road on towards the holy place. Though some came in luxurious automobiles, gliding swiftly along the road, continually sounding their horns, oxcarts dragged slowly alongside them. There were carriages of all types, victoria chaises, landaus, and wagons fitted out for the occasion with seats and crowded to the limit.

"Almost all brought besides food, a bundle of straw for the animals, which the poor man of Assisi called our brothers, and which carried out their tasks so bravely. Once in a while, one could see a small wagon trimmed with ornaments, small bells jingling softly as it moved along, yet the festive mood was discreet, manners were reserved, and the order perfect. Though little donkeys trotted along the side of the road, there were great numbers of

94

cyclists who had to perform real feats to keep from
tumbling.

"About ten in the morning, the skies became over-
cast. Soon it had turned to rain. Sheets of rain,
driven by a chilly fall wind, whipped the faces
of the pilgrims, drenched the roads, and chilled the
people to the bone. While some sought shelter under the trees, against the walls or in scattered
houses, others continued their march with impressive endurance.

"The road to Leiria dominates to a great extent
the wastes of Fátima where it is said the Virgin
appeared to the little shepherds. Parked along this
road were the carriages of the pilgrims and the
sightseers. The majority of the pilgrims, the thousands that came from many miles around and from
the provinces, gathered about the small holmoak,
which, in the words of the children, the Vision chose
for her pedestal. This was the center of a great
circle around which the devout and other spectators
ranged themselves."

Some estimated the crowd at the Cova da Iria
this day to be at least seventy thousand persons.
A professor of the University of Coimbra, Dr.
Almeida Garret, after careful consideration, placed
the number at over one hundred thousand. "There
were so many people there even on the twelfth,"
said Senhora da Capelinha, "that the din could be
heard even in our hamlet. The people spent the
whole night in the open since there was no shelter
for them. Before the sun rose they were already
up, praying, weeping and singing. I came very early
and was able to get close to the holmoak. The trunk
was the only thing left of it but I had adorned it
the night before with flowers and ribbons."

Away at Lúcia's home, everyone was disturbed. Senhora Santos was sad as she never had been before. She feared that this was Lúcia's last day on earth. Tears running down her face, she looked at her daughter who tried to cheer her.

"Don't fear, *maĩsinha*, little mother," Lúcia said with a caress, "for nothing will happen to us. Our Lady shall do what she promised."

When Lúcia was ready, Senhora Santos decided to go also, "for if my daughter dies, I want to be at her side." Accompanied by her husband, she took Lúcia to Jacinta's house.

The house overflowed with people; scores upon scores pressed outside, waiting for the children. "The curious and the devout filled the house to the limit," Ti Marto recalls. "It rained hard and the road was a mire; it was all a thick slime. My wife was worried. There were people over the beds and the trunks, soiling everything. 'My dear, don't let it bother you,' I calmed her. 'When the house is full no one else can come in.' When the time came for me to leave after the children, a neighbor took me aside and said in my ear, 'Marto, you'd better not go for you may be mistreated. The children, as they are only children, no one will hurt them. But you are in danger of being harmed.' 'As to me,' I replied, 'I'm going in my good faith. I'm not afraid at all. I've no doubt as to the good outcome.' My Olimpia was very frightened, practically at her wit's end, recommending herself to Our Lady. She awaited the worst, as priests and many others presaged only evil.

"The children were as much at ease as they could be. Francisco and Jacinta hadn't a care in the world. 'Look,' said Jacinta, 'if they hurt us, we'll go to

96

Heaven, but pity them, for they shall go to Hell.'

"A lady from Pombalinho, no less than the Baroness of Almeirim, had brought two dresses for the girls, a blue one for Lúcia and a white one for Jacinta. She dressed them herself and placed garlands of artificial flowers on their heads. It made them look like little angels. We left the house under torrents of rain. The road was oozing mud but it did not keep the women and even the fine ladies from kneeling before the children. 'Don't do that, women!' I had to repeat. They believed that the children had the power of the saints.

"After many struggles and interruptions, we came at last to the Cova da Iria. The crowds were so thick that it was difficult to pierce through them. It was then that a chauffeur took my Jacinta in his arms and, pushing along, opened a way to the posts with the lanterns, continually shouting, 'make way for the children who have seen Our Lady.'

"I followed them close, but Jacinta seeing me pressed among the people, feared for me. 'Don't push my father,' she broke out, 'don't push my father.'

"The man set Jacinta on the ground near the holmoak, but the crush there was so great that the child began to cry. Francisco and Lúcia placed her between themselves.

"My Olimpia was on the other side, I don't know where, but my comadre, Maria Rosa Santos, was close by the children. I was a little distance away and suddenly became aware of a fiendish looking man bearing down on my shoulder with his staff. 'The trouble begins,' I said to myself. The multitude swayed back and forth until the moment came when everyone stood still and quiet. The time

97

had come for the apparition, it was noon by the sun."

"There was a priest close by," Senhora da Capelinha tells, "who had spent the night near the holm-oak and he was saying his breviary. When the children arrived, dressed as if for First Communion, he asked them about the time of the apparition. 'At noon,' Lúcia responded. The priest took out his watch and said, 'Look, it is already noon. Our Lady never lies. Let us wait.' A few minutes went by. He looked at his watch again. 'Noon is gone. Everyone out of here! The whole thing is an illusion!'

"Lúcia did not want to leave so the priest began pushing the three children away. Lúcia, almost in tears, said, 'Whoever wants may go away. I'm not going. I'm on my own property. Our Lady said she was coming. She always came before and so must be coming again.' Just then, she glanced towards the east and said to Jacinta, 'Jacinta, kneel down; Our Lady is coming. I've seen the flash.' The priest was silenced. I never saw him again." The hour of the apparition had arrived; the miracle that was promised had begun to take place.

X. *Sixth Apparition*
(continued)

"SILENCE, silence, Our Lady is coming," Lúcia cried out as she saw the flash. The rain having ceased, the sun began gradually to appear, and Our Lady came. Her snow white feet rested upon the beautiful flowers and ribbons with which Senhora da Capelinha had adorned the tree. The faces of the three children assumed an unworldly expression, their features becoming more delicate, their color mellow, their eyes intent upon the Lady. They did not hear Lúcia's mother warning her to look closely so as not to be deceived. "What do you want of me?" Lúcia inquired of the Queen of Heaven.

"I want to tell you that they must build a chapel here in my honor; that I am the Lady of the Rosary; that they continue to say the Rosary every day. The war will end and the soldiers will return to their homes soon," Our Lady responded.

"I have many favors to ask. Do you wish to grant them or not?"

"Some I will! Others I will not! They must mend their lives, ask forgiveness for their sins. Offend not Our Lord any more," Our Lady continued, her face becoming very grave, *"For He is already much offended."*

Lúcia, knowing this was to be the last interview with Our Lady, wanted to make sure that she received all the commands Mary wished to give her. She hoped to spend the rest of her life on earth fulfilling the desires of Our Lady. "Do you want anything else from me?" the girl asked.

"I desire nothing else."

As Our Lady took leave of the children, she opened her hands which emitted a flood of light. While she was rising, she pointed towards the sun and the light gleaming from her hands brightened the sun itself.

"There she goes; there she goes," shouted Lúcia, without for a moment taking her eyes from the beautiful Queen of Heaven. Lúcia did not afterwards remember having said these words, though Fran-

99

cisco and Jacinta and many others distinctly heard her. Lúcia said later that she had no recollection of it. "I was not even aware of the presence of the people. My purpose was not to call the attention of the people to it; I did it, carried away by an interior movement which impelled me to it."

The echo of Lúcia's shout came back in a huge, immense cry of wonder and astonishment from the multitude. The sun was now pale as the moon. To the left of the sun, Saint Joseph appeared holding in his left arm the Child Jesus. Saint Joseph emerged from the bright clouds only to his chest, sufficient to allow him to raise his right hand and make, together with the Child Jesus, the Sign of the Cross three times over the world. As Saint Joseph did this, Our Lady stood in all her brilliancy to the right of the sun, dressed in the blue and white robes of Our Lady of the Rosary.

Meanwhile, Francisco and Jacinta were bathed in the marvellous colors and signs of the sun, and Lúcia was privileged to gaze upon Our Lord dressed in red as the Divine Redeemer, blessing the world, as Our Lady had foretold. Like Saint Joseph, He was seen only from His chest up. Beside Him stood Our Lady, dressed now in the purple robes of Our Lady of Sorrows, but without the sword. Finally, the Blessed Virgin appeared again to Lúcia in all her ethereal brightness, clothed in the simple brown robes of Mount Carmel.[7]

As the children stared enraptured by these most beautiful heavenly visions, the countless thousands

[7] "I cannot give details of this apparition; it took place on the thirteenth of October, at the height of the sun and in a change of light that took on an aspect that gave us the understanding that she showed herself as such: Our Lady of Carmel." (Lúcia, March, 1947.)

of people were amazed and overpowered by other miracles in the skies. The sun had taken on an extraordinary color. The words of eye-witnesses best describe these stupendous signs. "We could look at the sun with ease," Ti Marto testified; "it did not bother at all. It seemed to be continually fading and glowing in one fashion, then another. It threw shafts of light one way and another painting everything in different colors, the people, the trees, the earth, even the air. But the greatest proof of the miracle was the fact that the sun did not bother the eyes." A man like Ti Marto who spent all of his days in the open fields with his flocks and tended his garden under the hot sun of the Portuguese hills, marvelled at this fact. "Everybody stood still and quiet, gazing at the sun," he went on. "At a certain point, the sun stopped its play of light and then started dancing. It stopped once more and again started dancing until it seemed to loosen itself from the skies and fall upon the people. It was a moment of terrible suspense."

Maria da Capelinha gave the author her impressions of this tremendous miracle. "The sun cast different colors, yellow, blue and white. It trembled constantly. It looked like a revolving ball of fire falling upon the people." As the sun hurled itself towards the earth in a mighty zigzag motion, the multitude cried out in terror, "Ai Jesús, we are all going to die here; Ai Jesús, we are all going to die here." Some begged for mercy, "Our Lady save us;" many others made acts of contrition. One lady was even confessing her sins aloud.

At last the sun swerved back to its orbit and rested in the sky. "Everyone gave a sigh of relief;

we were still alive, and the miracle promised by the children had come to pass."

Our Lord already so much offended by the sins of mankind and particularly by the mistreatment of the children by the officials of the county, could easily have destroyed the world on that eventful day. However, Our Lord did not come to destroy, but to save. He saved the world that day through the blessing of good Saint Joseph and the love of the Immaculate Heart of Mary for her children on earth. Our Lord would have stopped the great World War then raging and given peace to the world through Saint Joseph, Jacinta later declared, if the children had not been arrested and taken to Ourem. "What you do to these my least brethren," warns Our Lord, "you do to Me."

The miracle had come to pass at the hour and day designated by Our Lady. No one was disappointed, no one but Our Lady, perhaps, who said the miracle would have been much greater if the children had not been so mistreated. Many thousands of people in the Cova da Iria and in neighboring villages witnessed the overwhelming signs. Their reports are of intense interest. There are slight variations in their descriptions of the events, though all agreed it was the most tremendous, the most awe-inspiring sight they ever witnessed. Some idea can be had of its effect on the people by reading the newspaper accounts of the day.

"At one o'clock, the hour of the sun, the rain stopped," *"O Dia"* reported. "The sky had a certain greyish tint of pearl and a strange clearness filled the gloomy landscape, every moment getting gloomier. The sun seemed to be veiled with transparent gauze to enable us to look at it without difficulty.

The greyish tint of mother-of-pearl began changing as if into a shining silver disc, that was growing slowly until it broke through the clouds. And the silvery sun, still shrouded in the same greyish lightness of gauze, was seen to rotate and wander within the circle of the receded clouds! The people cried out with one voice, the thousands of the creatures of God whom faith raised up to Heaven, fell to their knees upon the muddy ground.

"Then as if it were shining through the stained glass windows of a great cathedral, the light became a rare blue, spreading its rays upon the gigantic nave. . . . Slowly the blue faded away and now the light seemed to be filtered through yellow stained glass. Yellow spots were falling now upon the white kerchiefs and the dark poor skirts of coarse wool. They were spots which repeated themselves indefinitely over the lowly holmoaks, the rocks and the hills. All the people were weeping and praying bareheaded, weighed down by the greatness of the miracle expected. These were seconds, moments, that seemed hours; they were so fully lived."

"*O Seculo,*" another newspaper of Lisbon, carried a more detailed account of the extraordinary events. "From the height of the road where the people parked their carriages and where many hundreds stood, afraid to brave the muddy soil, we saw the immense multitude turn towards the sun at its highest, free of all clouds. The sun called to mind a plate of dull silver. It could be stared at without the least effort. It did not burn or blind. It seemed that an eclipse was taking place. All of a sudden a tremendous shout burst forth, 'Miracle, miracle! Marvel, marvel!'

"Before the astonished eyes of the people, whose

attitude carried us back to biblical times, and who, white with terror, heads uncovered, gazed at the blue sky, the sun trembled and made some brusque unheard-of movements beyond all cosmic laws; the sun danced, in the typical expression of the peasants.

"On the running board of the bus from Torres Novas, an old man whose stature and gentle, manly features recall those of Paul Deroulède, turned toward the sun and recited the *Credo* in a loud voice. . . . I saw him later addressing those about him who still kept their hats on, begging them vehemently to take their hats off before this overwhelming demonstration of the existence of God. Similar scenes were repeated at other places. A lady, bathed in tears and almost choking with grief, sobbed, 'How pitiful! There are men who still do not bare their heads before such a stupendous miracle!'

"Immediately afterwards the people asked each other if they saw anything and what they had seen. The greatest number avowed that they saw the sun trembling and dancing; others declared that they saw the smiling face of the Blessed Virgin herself; they swore that the sun turned around on itself as if it were a wheel of fireworks and had fallen almost to the point of burning the earth with its rays. Some said they saw it change colors successively."

The testimony of another witness, Dr. Almeida Garret, professor at the University of Combra, is most informative and corroborates the others. "As I waited," he said, "with cool and serene expectation, looking upon the place of the apparitions and with a curiosity that was fading because the hour was passing away so slowly without anything to arouse my attention, I heard the rustle of thousands of voices. I saw the people stretched out over the large field turn about from the point upon which their desires and anxieties had converged so far to the opposite side and they looked up to the skies. It was almost two o'clock wartime or about noon, sun time.

"The sun had broken jubilantly through the thick layer of clouds just a few moments before. It was shining clearly and intensely. I turned to this magnet that was drawing all eyes. It looked to me as a luminous and brilliant disc, with a bright well-defined rim. It did not hurt the eyes. The comparison (which I heard while still at Fátima) with a disc of dull silver, did not seem right to me. The color was brighter, far more active and richer than dull silver, with the tinted luster of the orient of a pearl.

"Nor did it resemble the moon on a clear night. Everyone saw and felt that it was a body with life. It was not spheric like the moon, neither did it have an equal tonality of color. It looked like a small, brightly polished wheel of irridescent mother-of-pearl. It could not be taken for the sun as though seen through fog. There was no fog at that time. (The rain and the fog had stopped.) The sun was not opaque, veiled or diffused. It gave light and heat and was brightly outlined by a beveled rim. The sky was banked with light clouds, patched with blue here and there. Sometimes the sun stood out alone in rifts of clear sky. The clouds scuttled along from west to east without dimming the sun. They gave the impression of passing behind it, while the white puffs gliding sometimes in front of the sun seemed to take on the color of rose or a delicate blue.

"It was a wonder that all this time it was possible for us to look at the sun, a blaze of light and burning heat, without any pain to the eyes or blinding of the retina. This phenomenon must have lasted about ten minutes, except for two interruptions when the sun darted forth its more refulgent, lightning-like rays, that forced us to look away.

"The sun had an eccentricity of movement. It was not the scintillation of a celestial body at its highest power. It was rotating upon itself with exceedingly great speed. Suddenly, the people broke out with a cry of extreme anguish. The sun, still rotating, had unloosened itself from the skies and came hurtling towards the earth. This huge, fiery millstone threatened to crush us with its weight. It was a dreadful sensation.

"During this solar occurrence, the air took on successively different colors. While looking at the sun, I noticed that everything around me darkened. I looked at what was nearby and cast my eyes away towards the horizon. Everything had the color of an amethyst: the sky, the air, everything and everybody. A little oak nearby was casting a heavy purple shadow on the ground.

"Fearing impairment of the retina, which was improbable, because then I would not have seen everything in purple, I turned about, closed my eyes, cupping my hands over them, to cut off all light. With my back turned, I opened my eyes and realized that the landscape and the air retained the purple hue.

"This did not give the impression of being an eclipse. While still looking at the sun, I noticed that the air had cleared and I heard a peasant nearby say, 'This lady looks yellow.' As a matter of fact, everything far and near had changed now. People seemed to have jaundice. I smiled when I saw everybody looking disfigured and ugly. My hand had the same color . . ."

The testimony of this learned man demonstrates how difficult it is to describe adequately the marvellous signs that occurred in the skies on this day. October the thirteenth, 1917, was a day to remember for all the people who witnessed these events. The reporter for the *Ordem,* a newspaper of Oporto, wrote about it in these words. "The sun was sometimes surrounded by blood-red flames, at other times it was aureoled with yellow and soft purple; again it seemed to be possessed of the swiftest rotation and then seemed to detach itself from the heavens, come near the earth and give forth a tremendous heat."

Another witness, the Reverend Manuel da Silva, wrote a letter to a friend the evening of the thirteenth in which he tried to describe the events of the day. He spoke about the morning's rain and then, "immediately the sun came out with a well-defined rim and seemed to come down to the height of the clouds. It started to rotate intermittently around itself like a wheel of fireworks, for about eight minutes. Everything became almost dark and the people's features became yellow. All were kneeling in the mud."

Inácio Lourenço was a boy nine years old at the time, living in the village of Alburitel, ten miles away from Fátima. He is now a priest and he remembers this day vividly. He was in school. "About noon," he said, "we were startled by the cries and exclamations of the people going by the school. The teacher was the first to run outside to the street with all the children following her. The people cried and wept on the street; they were all pointing towards the sun. It was 'The Miracle' promised by Our Lady.

107

I feel unable to describe it as I saw it and felt it
at the time. I was gazing at the sun; it looked so
pale to me, it did not blind. It was like a ball of
snow rotating upon itself. All of a sudden, it seemed
to be falling, zigzag, threatening the earth. Seized
with fear, I hid myself amidst the people. Everyone
was crying, waiting for the end of the world.

"Nearby, there was a godless man who had spent
the morning making fun of the simpletons who had
gone to Fátima just to see a girl. I looked at him
and he was numbed, his eyes riveted on the sun.
I saw him tremble from head to foot. Then he
raised his hands towards Heaven, as he was kneeling
there in the mud, and cried out, 'Our Lady, Our
Lady.' Everyone was crying and weeping, asking God
to forgive them their sins. After this was over, we
ran to the chapels, some to one, others to the other
one in our village. They were soon filled.

"During the minutes that the miracle lasted,
everything around us reflected all the colors of the
rainbow. We looked at each other and one seemed
blue, another yellow, red and so on. It increased the
terror of the people. After ten minutes, the sun
resumed its place, as pale, and without splendor.
When everyone realized the danger was over, there
was an outburst of joy. Everyone broke out in a
hymn of praise to Our Lady."

As the miracle came to its end and the people
arose from the muddy ground, another surprise
awaited them. A few minutes before, they had been
standing in the pouring rain, soaked to the skin. Now
they noticed that their clothes were perfectly dry.
How kind was Our Lady to her friends who had
braved rain and mud, and put on their very best
clothes for her visit.

108

The Bishop of Leiria wrote in his Pastoral Letter that those who witnessed the events of this great day were fortunate indeed. "The children long before set the day and hour at which it was to take place," he said. "The news spread quickly over the whole of Portugal and although the day was chilly and pouring rain, many thousands of people gathered. . . . They saw the different manifestations of the sun paying homage to the Queen of Heaven and Earth, who is more radiant than the sun in all its splendor. This phenomenon which no astronomical observatory registered was not natural. It was seen by people of all classes, members of the Church and non-Catholics. It was seen by reporters of the principal newspapers and by people many miles away." These are his official words, spoken after long study and careful interrogations of many witnesses of the apparition. There is no possibility of error or illusion when close to a hundred thousand people concur in their testimony. God in Heaven had called the people of the world to join with the heavens in paying honor and glory to His Blessed Mother, Mary.

XI. Francisco Leads the Way

WHAT IS OFTEN OVERLOOKED by those who read of Fátima now is the fact that for years nothing was revealed of the content of the revelations as given in the foregoing pages. Only the urgency to pray and do penance, and the promise of a miracle, were mentioned by the children.

After the first apparition of Our Lady the children pledged one another to secrecy for fear of being ridiculed. But since the message of Fátima was intended by Our Lord not merely for the children but for the whole world, God used Jacinta's enthusiasm to make known the fact of the apparition to the world. After the second apparition, however, that of June 13th, their secrecy was of a different order. As Lúcia says in her Memoirs, "When we said (before the apparition of July the 13th) that Our Lady had revealed a secret to us, we referred to this (reparation to the Immaculate Heart). Our Lady did not tell us at this time to keep (this revelation) secret, but we felt that God moved us to it." (Memoirs, Dec. 8, 1941) This inclination of the children to silence was confirmed by Our Lady when, on July the 13th, she told them what Lúcia calls, and what is known as, the Secret proper. It was only after many years that any of the substance of this secret revelation was made known by Lúcia; and even to this date there are important words of Our Lady yet undisclosed.

After the last apparition on October 13th, 1917, the three children tried to return to their ordinary routine life; Francisco and Jacinta to await the day when Mary would come to take them to Heaven; Lúcia hoping soon to begin her work of spreading devotion and love for the Immaculate Heart of Mary. Henceforth, however, they were marked children, marked by men as well as by God. People flocked to see and speak with them, the poor, the rich, even priests came. They asked a thousand different questions, but the answers were always the same. The innocence, seriousness and simplicity of the three were solid proof to both learned and unlearned alike of their utter truthfulness. To see them was to believe in them.

Francisco testified that he saw Our Lady, that her radiant beauty was blinding to the eyes, but that he never heard her speak. Jacinta could tell more, but she candidly admitted that sometimes she had not heard Our Lady very well and had forgotten many things. If the people wanted to know more, they should ask Lúcia. Lúcia would repeat the story word for word every time; but sometimes and in fact very often people would try to make her reveal the secret of the revelations. Then Jacinta and Lúcia kept silence sometimes to the point of being impolite. What saddened them and confused them terribly was when priests came and tried to pry the secret out of them. They did not want to be rude with God's priests, yet they felt they had to keep the secret.

Mary helped them in their dilemma. The Reverend Faustino Ferreira, pastor of the neighboring village and dean of the district, met them on one of his official visitations, and thenceforth seized every opportunity of speaking with them. The children were very much drawn to this priest since they were free to ask him all the questions they wanted to ask. They loved him for his kind ways and they followed his counsels faithfully. He was never too busy for them and would put their minds at ease about everything. He well realized that it was not so much his words that were influencing the children as the Mother of God. She was the artist, gently though firmly moulding their souls to the model of her First Born, the Child Jesus.

Our Lady had instructed Francisco, through Lúcia, that she would take him to heaven soon, but that he must say many Rosaries. He never forgot these words and like Saint Dominic, he became a real apostle of the Rosary. He had no other interest in life than to fulfill these words of Our Lady of the Rosary. One day, two fine ladies came to his house and asked him what he would like to be when he grew up.

"Do you want to be a carpenter?"

"No, ma'am."

"A soldier?"

"No."

"A doctor? Wouldn't you like to be a good doctor?"

"No."

"I know what you would like to be, a priest! You would like to say Mass, hear confessions, and give sermons. Is that it?"

"No, ma'am, I don't want to be a priest either."

"Then what do you want to be?"

"I don't want to be anything. I just want to die and go to Heaven."

Francisco's father, who was listening to this conversation, said,

"That is really his heart's desire."

Francisco took to separating himself from Lúcia and Jacinta after they reached the hills. More and more he appeared to want to meditate on all that Our Lady had told the children. He would say afterwards: "I liked to see the Angel so much, but I liked Our Lady much more. What I liked best about the apparitions was seeing Our Lord in that light that the Blessed Virgin put into our hearts. I love God very much. He is so sad because of so many sins. We must not commit even the smallest sin."

The children gradually gave up all thoughts of

112

play. Sometimes in the company of the others they would sing and dance as usual, but only so as not to appear singular. Jacinta and Francisco, knowing they were soon to die, gave themselves more and more to mortification and prayer. They could not get interested in school because to them it served no purpose. It was but time wasted, when they could be spending it more profitably in the presence of Our Lord in the Eucharist.

Both of them had made their first Confession in the year of the apparitions, but their First Communion was deferred for another year. When the time came for them to receive the Eucharist, Francisco failed to pass the catechism test, and so he had to wait longer. So heartbroken was the poor boy when his sister approached the altar rail that he could not enter the church. He remained outside, leaning against the stones of the church sobbing his eyes out.

Although the public apparitions ended with that of October 13th, Our Lady by no means abandoned the three chosen ones after that. We have it on Jacinta's testimony to her pastor that three times in the following year she appeared to the little girl; and as we shall see later on, she continued to appear to Lúcia, long after her childhood. Moreover, the power of Our Lady of Fátima was manifest in the favors granted through the special intercession of the children. To cite but one instance, there was the man for whose safe return home Jacinta was asked to pray. The man, who had just escaped from jail and was tramping aimlessly about, found himself quite hopelessly lost in the hills and in great distress at the time of Jacinta's intercession. Kneeling down on the ground to pray, he saw Jacinta standing before him. The little child led him safely to the road home and then vanished from his sight. Jacinta, however, had no knowledge of the remarkable incident until the man returned to report it.

Of Lúcia's power little is known since she is reluctant to discuss herself in that way. But it is an established fact that her mother was brought remarkably through a grave illness through Lúcia's faith in Our Lady. The requests placed before the children for prayers were endless, and the wonderful answers to their prayers attest to the favor in which they stood before the Mother of God.

Towards the end of October, 1918, the whole Marto family came down with influenza. The father alone escaped, so he was able to take care of the rest. He could not do his ordinary work for he had to take care of the house, cook the meals, and watch over each one of his large family. "I was bowed down with heavy burdens," he said, "but the finger of God was in this. He helped me. I never had to borrow money. There was always enough."

Francisco was in a very serious condition. He could not move out of bed. At this time, Our Lady appeared to Francisco and Jacinta, telling them that she would come for Francisco very soon and that Jacinta would follow him not long after. They were so happy at this good news that Jacinta confided in her cousin, "Look, Lúcia, Our Lady came to see us and said that she was coming soon for Francisco. She asked me if I still wanted to convert more sinners. I said yes. Our Lady wants me to go to two hospitals but it is not to cure me. It is to suffer more for the love of God, the conversion of sinners and in reparation for the offenses committed against the Immaculate Heart of Mary. She told me that

114

you would not go with me. My mother will take me there and afterwards I am to be left there alone." How courageous was this little girl to offer herself as a victim of love and reparation to God and Mary.

Francisco had this selfsame spirit of love and sacrifice. He was a very sick boy and some of the medicines he had to take were not particularly agreeable. "Yet he would take any medicine we gave him," his mother said. "He never fussed. I could never find out what he liked. If I gave him a glass of milk, he took it; and when I gave him an egg, he sucked it. Poor child! He took any bitter medicine without making a face. This gave us hope that he would recover, but he always repeated that it was useless since Our Lady was going to come for him. He knew well what was in store for him."

Francisco improved enough to allow him to take short walks, and he always turned his steps towards the Cova da Iria. Once there, he would kneel near the stump of the holmoak, his eyes seeking the blue sky beyond which dwelt Our Lady. His eyes sparkled with new life as he thought of the joy that would soon be his when Our Lady came to take him up to Heaven. He would return from the Cova da Iria somewhat refreshed; so much so that his father said, "You are going to get better. You are going to grow up to be a fine big man."

"Our Lady will come soon for me," he replied with utter certitude.

Tired and saddened by the long vigils of caring for his sick family, the father would reply, "God's will be done." And tears would burst from his eyes.

Francisco's godmother once said, "If Our Lady

will cure you, I promise to offer your weight in wheat."

"That is useless. Our Lady will not do you this favor." Francisco was right. As the days went on, he lost the strength to get up from his bed. He was sinking very fast under the weight of a persistently high fever. However, his ready smile and continual cheerfulness misled everyone as to his true condition.

The influenza epidemic did not by-pass Lúcia's family. Most of them were taken sick though Lúcia was spared. She helped nurse the sick in her family and every chance she had, she ran over to the Marto house to see if she could help them, but especially she wanted to be with Francisco and Jacinta. She knew they would leave her soon. She divided her time between their two rooms. Sitting on a footstool next to their beds, she exchanged with them the confidences of their hearts.

"Have you made any sacrifices today?" Lúcia asked Jacinta.

"I have made a lot. My mother went out and many times I wanted to get out of bed and go to Francisco's room but I didn't."

Lúcia told Jacinta what she herself was able to do to prove her love for Our Lady. She told about her little prayers and sacrifices. "I did that too," little Jacinta spoke up. "I love Our Lord and Our Lady and I never get tired of telling Them that I love Them. When I tell that to Them, it seems sometimes that I have a fire burning in my breast, a fire that does not consume. . . . Oh, how I would like to be able to go again to the hills to say the Rosary in the Cave. But I can't any more. When you go to the Cova da Iria, pray for me, Lúcia!

I'm sure I'll never go there again. Now you go to Francisco's room because I want to make the sacrifice of being alone."

As she sat next to Francisco's bed, Lúcia gently whispered to him, "Francisco, are you suffering a great deal?"

"Yes, I am. I suffer it all for the love of Our Lord and Our Lady. I want to suffer more and I can't." He lifted himself up a little to see if the door was closed tight. He fumbled under the pillow for his rope of penance and handed it to Lúcia. "You keep it for me. I'm afraid mother will see it. If I get up again, I want it back." Our Lady had told them that God did not want them wearing the rope in bed but they kept it nearby just in case they ever got up.

Francisco knew well that he would not recover. "Look, Lúcia, I'm going soon to Heaven. Jacinta is going to pray a great deal for sinners and for the Holy Father and for you. You're going to stay here below because Our Lady wants you to. Do whatever she wants."

"Jacinta seemed to be interested only in the conversion of sinners; she wanted to save people from Hell," Lúcia said later, "but Francisco's only desire was to console Our Lord and Our Lady Who seemed to him so sorrowful."

"I feel very sick," he confided to Lúcia, "but I'll be in Heaven soon."

"Then make sure you pray very much for sinners and for the Holy Father, Jacinta and me."

"Yes, I'll pray. But you should rather ask Jacinta for that. I'm afraid I'll forget everything when I see Our Lord. After all, I would rather console Jesus and Mary."

117

Lúcia's visits seemed to lighten the sorrows of sickness in the Marto home. "It made me sorry to watch Jacinta in bed, covering her face with her hands and not moving for hours at a time," said her mother. "She said she was thinking. When I asked her what she was thinking about, she smiled and said, 'Nothing, mother.' She kept no secrets, however, from her cousin Lúcia. Lúcia brought joy and happiness to everyone. When the two girls were alone, they talked continually and in such a way that none of us could catch a word of what they said no matter how hard we tried. When anyone went near them, they lowered their heads and kept quiet. No one could penetrate their mysterious confidences."

"What did Jacinta tell you?" Senhora Olimpia once asked Lúcia, as she was leaving for her home. Lúcia smiled and sped away. "But I do know that they used to say Rosary after Rosary, at least seven or eight every day and there was no end to their short prayers."

Francisco, however, in his last days, was not able to recite his prayers. "Mother, I can't say the Rosary, I can't even say the Hail Mary without being distracted."

"If you can't pray with your lips, do it with your heart. It will make Our Lord happy just the same." He understood and felt better.

As his fever rose and his appetite failed, he realized the end was near. "Father," he said to his dad, "before I die, I want to receive Our Lord." He had not yet received his First Holy Communion.

Francisco's words were a sword in the heart of his loving Father. He hated the thought of losing his little boy, but with manly courage he spoke up,

118

"I'll take care of that right away. I'll go right now to see the priest." The father remembered so well that sad journey. He tells how he took some of the other children with him and on the way back, they said their Rosary together, but because he forgot his beads, he had to count them on his fingers.

Meanwhile, Francisco called his sister Teresa and asked her to call Lúcia right away. When Lúcia came, he asked his mother and brothers to leave his room because he wanted to talk to Lúcia alone. When they went out he said, "Lúcia, I'm going to make my Confession now and die. I want you to tell me if you ever saw me commit any sins."

"Sometimes you disobeyed your mother when she wanted you to stay home. You sneaked away to be with me or to hide yourself."

"It's true. I committed that sin. Now go and ask Jacinta if she remembers any."

Lúcia went to ask her. After some thought Jacinta answered, "Yes, look. Tell him that before Our Lady appeared to us, he stole ten cents. And when the boys threw stones at the boys from Boleiros, he helped them."

Lúcia told this to Francisco and he said, "I have confessed those already, but I'll confess them again. Maybe they are the reason why Our Lord is so sad. As for me, even if I were not to die, I wouldn't do it again. I'm sorry. My Jesus, forgive us," he began to pray, joining his hands, "forgive us; save us from the fire of Hell." Then turning to Lúcia again, "Look, Lúcia, you too ask Our Lord to forgive me my sins."

"I will, don't worry. If Our Lord had not forgiven you, Our Lady would not have told Jacinta that she

119

was coming for you soon. I'm going to go to Mass to pray for you."

That afternoon, the priest came to hear Francisco's Confession and promised to bring him his First Holy Communion in the morning. He was so happy and he asked his mother to be sure not to give him anything to eat or drink after midnight. He wanted to fast like everyone else. The next morning, when he heard the tinkling of the bell announcing the coming of Our Lord, he tried to sit up in bed but his strength failed him and he fell back on the pillow. He received Jesus into his heart, closed his eyes in prayer, abiding in Jesus as He abode in him. As the feeling of the presence of God pervaded him, he recalled that other day when the Angel came and together they adored Jesus in the Blessed Sacrament. This faithful boy had given his life to make reparation to the Hearts of Jesus and Mary for the sins of men. He had spent hours, whole days, dreaming of his loved Ones, Jesus and Mary, scorning the absorbing pleasures of childhood to comfort their loving Hearts. With Christ within him, Francisco offered himself again and again as a victim of love, consolation and reparation. He finally opened his eyes and saw his mother tearfully looking upon him. He said, "Mother, will the priest bring me Communion again tomorrow?" But this was his first and last Communion; tomorrow he would be with Jesus and Mary in Heaven.

Lúcia came to attend Francisco's First Communion. Jacinta also was allowed to get up and visit with her brother. "I can't pray anymore," he confided to them, "you pray for me." The two girls knelt and prayed. "Lúcia, maybe I'm going to miss

120

you very much. I'd like Our Lord to take you to Heaven very soon."

"You're going to miss me? Oh no! As if it were possible when you are near Our Lord and Our Lady Who are so good."

"You are right. Maybe I won't remember you."

Francisco lingered on until evening, failing faster every minute. He was extremely thirsty. Lúcia and his mother, staying faithfully with him, tried occasionally to give him a spoonful of water, but he was too weak even to swallow. They asked him how he felt. To spare his mother worry and grief, he managed to say, "I'm fine. I've got no pains." But when he was alone with Lúcia and Jacinta, they realized what he was going through; it gave him much relief to open up his heart to them. "I'm going to go to Heaven, and I'm going to ask Our Lord and Our Lady to take you there soon."

"Give my best wishes, my very best wishes to Our Lord and to Our Lady," Jacinta interrupted, "and tell Them that I'll suffer all that They want me to, for the conversion of sinners and in reparation for the sins committed against the Immaculate Heart of Mary."

His mother came in to watch over her little boy. Though her constant prayer was "God's will be done," it did not lessen the sorrow of her heart as she watched little Francisco die before her eyes. All was darkness on the hills and in the Marto home. Suddenly Francisco aroused himself to speak, "Mother, look! What a beautiful light—by the door!" His eyes opened wide with new life. "Now it's gone; I can't see it anymore."

Morning came; the end would come any moment. He asked them all to bless him, pray for him and

to please forgive him all his faults. Their eyes filled
with tears as they said they would. About ten, as
the morning sun shone brightly into the room, his
face brightened, an angelic smile parted his lips as
he breathed his last breath. Without any agony,
with utmost peace, he made his exit from this world.
This boy had finished the work God had given him
to do. Friday morning, the fourth day of April, in
the year 1919, Our Lady came to claim him for her
own.

The following day, his mortal remains were taken
to the cemetery in prayerful procession. First there
was the crucifix, followed by a group of men dressed
in green robes, then the priest, while behind the
priest, four boys in white robes carried the body.
Lúcia and the Marto family with many friends
walked along, tears streaming from their saddened
eyes. Little Jacinta was so sick she had to stay at
home in bed. A simple wooden cross was placed over
his grave. As long as Lúcia remained in the village,
never a day went by without her going to visit the
grave of her beloved Francisco. She knew he was
happy with Jesus and Mary in Heaven and that he
would not forget his promise always to pray for
Jacinta and herself. Nothing could separate them on
earth and nothing would separate them in death.

XII. *Jacinta's Death*

FRANCISCO'S DEATH left Lúcia and Jacinta utterly
heartbroken. Though they realized he was happy in
Heaven with Our Lord and Our Lady, they missed

him. Their three hearts were as one and in losing
him, they felt they lost part of their heart. Jacinta
particularly was lonely for her brother. She would
sit up in bed, her head burning with fever, and remain motionless for hours, her face showing her
awful dejection.

"What are you thinking about, Jacinta?" her
mother asked.

"I'm thinking of Francisco. How much I would
love to see him." Jacinta could not tell everything
that was in her thoughts to her mother, though she
did confide in Lúcia. "I think of Francisco and how
I'd love to see him. But I think also of the war that
is going to come. So many people will die and so
many will go to Hell. Many cities shall be burned
to the ground and many priests will be killed. Look,
Lúcia, I'm going to Heaven. But when you see that
night lightened by that strange light, you also run
away to Heaven."

"Don't you see it's impossible to run away to
Heaven?"

"Yes, you can't do that. But don't be afraid. I'll
pray a lot for you in Heaven, and for the Holy
Father also, and for Portugal, for the war not to
come here and for all the priests."

Jacinta not only prayed, she suffered. The influenza from which she suffered grew worse daily and
an abscess formed on her chest. Her mother felt so
sad to see her dear little child in such pain but
Jacinta always came back with a consoling word.
"Don't worry, mother, for I'm going to Heaven. I'll
pray a lot for you there. Don't cry. I'm all right."
Little soldier that she was, she tried hard to forget
her sickness and pains so that she might console
her family and offer everything for the conversion

123

of sinners. "We must make many, many sacrifices and pray a lot for sinners," she confided to Lúcia, "so that no one shall ever again have to go to that prison of fire where people suffer so much." Jacinta did not let one moment of suffering go to waste. One twinge of pain was of more value to her than all the gold in the world.

A doctor came to her house and advised her parents to take her to the hospital at Ourem where she could get the best professional treatment. Jacinta knew that the best doctors in the world could not cure her. She was willing to go, however, in obedience to Our Lady, because it would give her a greater opportunity to sacrifice herself. Jacinta tried very hard to be courageous about going, but to go to a hospital and live among strangers, without her mother or father or her brothers and sisters was no easy sacrifice. The hardest thing of all, however, would be to say good-bye to Lúcia. How could she live without her!

"Lúcia," she whispered with tears in her eyes, "if only you could come with me! The hardest thing to me is to have to go without you. Maybe the hospital is a house that is very dark, where we can't see a thing! And I'll be there suffering all alone."

It had to be. Early in June, her good father lifted her frail body out of bed and placed her, as comfortably as possible, upon his little donkey. Together, they set out for the hospital in the town of Ourem.

Jacinta stayed in the hospital for two months under rigorous treatment. Once only did she have visitors, her mother and Lúcia. Lúcia tells about this visit. "I found her as happy as always to suffer for the love of God and the Immaculate Heart of Mary, for the conversion of sinners and for the Holy

124

Father. That was her ideal. That was all she spoke about."

They remained with Jacinta two days. Senhora Marto had to return to her family and Lúcia to hers though it tore their hearts to have to leave Jacinta in this distant hospital alone and among strangers. What made it even worse was the futility of it all. She was not improving, no matter how much the doctors did. The wound on her chest was large, open and continually running. Finally, the doctors agreed she might just as well be at home with her family and they discharged her towards the latter part of August.

"She was all bones," Father Formigão said, who visited her at home; "it was a shock to see how thin her arms were. She was running a fever all the time. Pneumonia, then tuberculosis and pleurisy ate away her strength. I remembered, as I saw her, that Our Lady had promised Bernadette of Lourdes that she too would not be happy in this world but in the next. I wondered if Our Lady made the same promise to Jacinta."

One day Jacinta confided to Lúcia, "When I'm alone, I get out of bed to say the Angel's prayer. Now I can't bow my head to the floor any more because I fall. I say it on my knees."

When Lúcia heard this, she thought she should talk it over with the Pastor of Olival. He advised Lúcia to tell Jacinta to say her prayers in bed.

"But will Our Lord like it?" Jacinta asked, still doubtful.

"Yes, He will. Our Lord wants us to do what the priest says."

"Then it's all right. I won't get up again for my

prayers." Jacinta would do what the priest of God advised.

Though she could not kneel to say her prayers, somehow or other, at times, Jacinta had enough strength to take a trip to the Cova da Iria. When winter came, her parents would not hear of her going to the Cova, but she prevailed upon them to allow her to go to Mass. She wanted to go every morning, as Lúcia did. "Don't come to Mass," Lúcia tried to counsel her, "it is too much for you. Besides, today isn't Sunday."

"That doesn't matter. I want to go in place of the sinners who don't go even on Sundays . . . Look, Lúcia, do you know? Our Lord is so sad and Our Lady told us that He must not be offended any more. He is already offended very much and no one pays any attention to it. They keep committing the same sins."

"Have you performed any other sacrifices, Jacinta?"

"Yes, Lúcia. Last night, I was very thirsty, but I did not drink anything. I felt a lot of pain and I offered Our Lord the sacrifice of not turning in bed. This is why I couldn't sleep. And you, Lúcia, have you performed any sacrifices today?" Lúcia's sacrifices were only for Jacinta's ears.

Lúcia tells another story about Jacinta. One day, Jacinta's mother brought her a glass of milk. "You drink this down, Jacinta; it is good for you."

"I don't want it, mother," she replied, pushing the glass away. Senhora Marto insisted but Jacinta would not give in.

"I don't know how I am going to make her take anything," her mother said, as she walked away.

When Senhora Marto had gone, Lúcia remon-

126

strated with Jacinta. "How does it happen that you disobey your mother! Aren't you going to offer that sacrifice to Our Lord?"

Hearing this, Jacinta's eyes filled with tears of sorrow. She called for her mother and asked to be forgiven. "I'll take anything you want me to take, mother." Her mother brought back the glass of milk and Jacinta took it without showing any sign of revulsion. Afterwards, as Lúcia was wiping away Jacinta's tears, the little girl confessed, "If you only knew how hard it was for me to drink it!"

From that time on, though Jacinta felt it increasingly difficult to drink milk or broth or to eat, she never flinched but tried bravely to take anything her mother gave her. One day, her mother brought in to her with the milk a bunch of grapes. Jacinta loved grapes, and her mother knew it would please her. "No, mother, I don't want the grapes. Take them away; just give me the milk." Later she confided to Lúcia, "I did want the grapes so much and it was so hard for me to drink that milk. But I preferred to offer a sacrifice."

Almost every day, on her way home from morning Mass and Communion, Lúcia would drop in to visit Jacinta. It was such a great joy to Jacinta. "Lúcia," she asked, "did you receive Communion today?"

"Yes, Jacinta."

"Then come very close to me for you have Our Lord in your heart. I don't know how it happens but I feel Our Lord in me and I understand what He says even if I don't see Him or hear Him. It is so good to be with Him."

Lúcia took from her prayerbook a little picture

of a chalice and Host. Jacinta took and kissed it so earnestly.

"It's the Hidden Jesus. I love Him so much. How I'd love to receive Him in church. Don't you take Communion in Heaven? If we do, I'll receive Him every day. If the Angel had come to the hospital to bring Communion to me, how happy I would have been."

Lúcia gave her a picture of the Sacred Heart of Jesus. She kept it with her all the time, day and night, and would kiss it frequently. "I kiss His Heart. It is the thing I love best. How I would like to have a picture of the Immaculate Heart of Mary. Don't you have any?"

"No, Jacinta, I can't find any."

"Soon I shall go to Heaven. You are to stay here to reveal that the Lord wants to establish throughout the world the devotion to the Immaculate Heart of Mary. When you start to reveal this, don't hesitate. Tell everyone that Our Lord grants us all graces through the Immaculate Heart of Mary; that all must make their petitions to her; that the Sacred Heart of Jesus desires that the Immaculate Heart of Mary be venerated at the same time. Tell them that they should all ask for peace from the Immaculate Heart of Mary, as God has placed it in her hands. Oh, if I could only put in the heart of everyone in the world the fire that is burning in me and makes me love so much the Heart of Jesus and the Heart of Mary."

Meanwhile, Our Lady did not leave her little patient alone. She visited Jacinta to say that she wanted her to go to another hospital in Lisbon. The little girl could hardly wait to tell Lúcia. "Lúcia, Our Lady told me that I'm going to go to another

128

hospital in Lisbon and that I'll never see you again
or my parents and that after suffering a great deal,
I shall die alone. She said that I should not be
afraid since she will come to take me with her to
Heaven." She reached out her tiny arms to embrace
Lúcia, saying between sobs, "I will never see you
again. Pray a lot for me for I am going to die
alone." The thought crushed the little child.

Once Lúcia found her embracing a picture of Our
Lady, praying aloud: "My dear little Mother, so I
am going to die alone?"

"Why do you worry about dying alone?" Lúcia
interrupted, hoping to distract her mind and cheer
her a bit. "What do you care when Our Lady is
going to come for you?"

"It's true. I don't care. I don't know why, but
sometimes I forget that she is going to come for
me."

"Take heart, Jacinta. You have only a little while
to wait before you go to Heaven. For me. . . ."
Lúcia's heart welled up with sorrow at the thought
of losing Jacinta so soon.

"Poor thing. Don't cry, Lúcia. I shall pray a lot
in Heaven for you. You are going to stay here, but
it is Our Lady who wants it."

"Jacinta, what are you going to do in Heaven?"

"I'm going to love Jesus a lot, and the Immaculate
Heart of Mary, and pray and pray for you, for the
Holy Father, my parents, brothers, sisters and for
everyone who asked me and for sinners. I love to
suffer for the love of Our Lord and Our Lady. They
love those who suffer for the conversion of sinners."

Everyone thought Jacinta was dreaming about going to the hospital in Lisbon. How would she get
there? What was the use? Her parents could not

129

afford it. Our Lady, however, had arranged everything.

Some few days after Jacinta announced that she was going to go to Lisbon, an automobile drove up in front of the Marto house. It was Father Formigão with two people, Doctor Eurico Lisboa and his wife. The doctor had heard about the happenings at the Cova da Iria and he wished to visit the holy place and speak with the children.

"Around the middle of January, 1920," the doctor stated, "we stopped at Santarem to see the Reverend Formigão who could inform us better than anyone else of the events that had taken place at Fátima. We went to the Cova da Iria with him and said the Rosary. Returning to Fátima, we stopped in to see Jacinta. She was pale and thin and walked with great difficulty. Her family was not upset about her condition as the only ambition of Jacinta was to go to Our Lady. I reproached them for not doing all in their power to help the girl. They answered that it was useless as Our Lady wanted to take her away and that she had already been at the hospital at Ourem and nothing could be done. I told them that the will of Our Lady is above human resources and that to make sure that Our Lady really wanted to take her, they should go to all lengths to save her.

"My words disturbed them so they asked the priest for his advice. He confirmed my words. Jacinta came to Lisbon on the second of February, 1920, where she was placed under the care of one of the leading specialists on children's diseases. The diagnosis was purulent pleurisy of the large left cavity, fistulous osteitis of the seventh and eighth ribs of the same side."

However, before Jacinta left Fátima for the hos-

pital, she begged her mother to take her once more to the Cova da Iria. "I decided to take Jacinta there on the donkey with the help of one of my friends. The child was so weak that she could not even stand. As we went by the bog of the Carreira, Jacinta got down from the donkey and began to say the Rosary alone. Then she picked some flowers to adorn the little Chapel. When we reached the Cova, we all knelt and she prayed for a while in her own way. After she got up, she said, 'When Our Lady went away, she passed over those trees and entered Heaven so fast that it seemed as if her feet were caught in the door.' "

The following day, Jacinta said good-bye to her beloved Lúcia. This was the bitterest cross of all for these two children; their hearts were one and it was like taking a sword and cutting their hearts in two. "She kept her arms around me for a long time," Lúcia wrote in her memoirs; "she was crying and saying to me, 'Never again shall we see each other. Pray a great deal for me for I am going to Heaven. There I will pray a lot for you. Don't ever tell anyone the secret even if they kill you. Love Jesus a great deal and the Immaculate Heart of Mary. Make many sacrifices for sinners.' "

The journey to Lisbon was a sad one for mother and child. Jacinta stayed at the window of the train all the while, admiring the countryside and the people in the villages they passed through. At Santarem, a lady who had heard about Jacinta's journey came to offer her a box of candy but the child would not touch a piece of it. When they reached Lisbon, some ladies met them and together they called on friends looking for a place to stay. No one would take a sick child. Jacinta appreciated well the sor-

132

row of the Immaculate Heart of Mary and of Saint Joseph when they went looking for a place to stay in the town of Bethlehem but "there was no room for them in the inn." Tired and disappointed, mother and daughter went to the orphanage of Our Lady of the Miracles and asked to be admitted. The Superior, Mother Maria da Purificação Godinho welcomed them with open arms. She had the highest regard for the little girl who had seen Our Lady.

While waiting in the parlor of the orphanage, a wealthy woman approached Jacinta and told the child about the trouble she was having with her eyes. She asked Jacinta to pray that her eyes might become better and she placed a two dollar bill in her hands. Jacinta did not speak and the lady went away discouraged. The child gave the money immediately to the Mother Superior who told her to give it to her mother. "No," Jacinta said, "this is for you. You are having so much trouble with me."

Later, the Superior asked the girl why she did not answer the lady. "Look, my dear Mother, I have prayed much for her. I didn't say anything then as I was afraid I might forget it, I had so many pains."

Senhora Marto remained at the orphanage for a few days to satisfy herself that Jacinta would be well taken care of. The Superior was a real mother to the child; she loved her dearly and Jacinta felt very much at home with all the children. What made the child's stay there especially happy was the fact that there was a chapel there. She was going to live in the same house with Jesus. Just as soon as she was admitted to the Orphanage, Jacinta wanted to be taken to the chapel. Every morning she received Communion. "On some occasions, when I was there,"

133

her mother related, "I carried her to the altar rail; while Mother Superior did on other occasions. I remember that she asked me if I would take her to a nearby church to go to Confession. We went before sunrise and on the way back all she could say was, 'what a nice priest; he was so kind. He asked me many things, so many things.' How I wanted to find out what the priest had asked her but Confession is not something for people to talk to each other about."

Jacinta spent every possible moment in the chapel kneeling, or when she could no longer kneel, she sat in the choir, her eyes riveted on the tabernacle. But in her ardent love for Jesus, she could not overlook the little discourtesies of visitors. "She saw some people who did not show proper reverence in the chapel," the Superior mentioned, "and she said to me, 'My dear Mother, don't allow that. They must act before the Blessed Sacrament as it is proper. Everyone must be quiet in church; they must not speak. If these poor people knew what is waiting for them!' I went downstairs to speak to the people who were misbehaving in the chapel, but I did not always have success. When I returned, she said, 'What happened?' I told her they would not listen. 'Patience,' she replied, her face showing her sorrow over the irreverences of the people, 'Our Lady is pleased with you. Will you tell the Cardinal? Yes? Our Lady does not want us to talk in church.'"

Often, the Superior would have Jacinta sit by the window which opened upon the park. It pleased the little girl to look at the trees moving in the breeze, to listen to the singing and chirping of the birds; it reminded her so much of Fátima, her parents, and especially of Lúcia. Jacinta fell in easily with the

134

other children; there were about twenty-five. She did not talk much, but there was one girl her own age whom she used to preach to at length. "It was funny to listen to her," the Superior remarked. " 'You must never tell a lie or be lazy, but be very obedient. Do everything well and with patience for the love of Our Lord if you want to go to Heaven!' She spoke with startling authority, as if she herself were not a little child."

"While she was with us, she was visited by Our Lady more than once," the Superior continued. "I remember once going into her room and standing at the foot of her bed. She said to me, her face radiant with beauty, 'Move over, please, dear Mother, because I am expecting Our Lady!' Sometimes it was not Our Lady, but a globe of light, as the one seen at Fátima, for then she would say, 'This time, it was not like up in Fátima, but I knew it was Our Lady.' "

After each visit of Our Lady, Jacinta spoke with wisdom far beyond her age, education or experience. "Who taught you so much?" the Superior once asked her, marvelling at her heavenly wisdom and insight.

"Our Lady taught me, but some things I think out myself. I like to think very much." She was so open and truthful in everything she said. The Mother Superior kept an account of all she said.

"Our Lady said that there are many wars and discords in the world. Wars are only punishments for the sins of the world. Our Lady cannot stay the arm of her Beloved Son upon the world anymore. It is necessary to do penance. If the people amend themselves, Our Lord shall still come to the aid of the world. If they do not amend themselves, punishment shall come."

In explaining this last statement of Jacinta's, the Superior wrote, "Jacinta is referring here to a calamity of which she had spoken privately. Our Lord is filled with anger against the sins and crimes committed in Portugal. A terrible social cataclysm threatens our country and above all, the city of Lisbon. Civil war will break out of a communist or anarchist nature, followed by looting, murder, fires and devastation of every sort. The capital will become the very image of Hell. When the offended Divine Justice shall inflict such a horrible punishment, everyone who can should flee from the city. This calamity, now foreboding, must be disclosed little by little and with discretion. 'Our Lady, how much I pity her. How much!' the child concluded."

Our Lady had revealed to this little child some terrible catastrophes that were in store for the world. "If people amend their lives," Jacinta said to Mother Godinho, "Our Lord will forgive the world, but if they do not, the punishment will come. If men do not amend their lives, Almighty God will send the world, beginning with Spain, a punishment such as never has been seen." She then spoke of "great world events that were to take place around the year 1940." The thought of these terrible misfortunes that men were bringing upon themselves through their hatred and disobedience to Our Lord and Our Lady filled the child with inconsolable sadness. It pained her more than her illness to realize the wicked way men were treating Jesus and Mary. "Oh, how sorry I am for Our Lady! How sorry!" she sobbed to Mother Godinho.

While Jacinta's mother was still there, Mother Godinho, the Superior, asked her if she would not like her two daughters, Florinda and Teresa, to become nuns. "God help me!" the mother protested, her heart heavy with sorrow over the death of Francisco and the impending death of Jacinta.

Jacinta did not hear her mother's words against the suggestion, but when the Superior came into her room later, the little girl commented, "Our Lady would have liked my sisters to become nuns very much. Mother does not want it and Our Lady will take them soon to Heaven." In fact, shortly after, the two girls died.

"You know, one thing I would love to do before I die would be to visit the Cova da Iria," the Superior once mentioned to Jacinta. It was a long journey and seemingly impossible.

"Don't worry, good Mother, you will go there after my death."

"My dear Mother, the sins that bring most souls to Hell are the sins of the flesh. Certain fashions are going to be introduced which will offend Our Lord very much. Those who serve God should not follow these fashions. The Church has no fashions; Our Lord is always the same. The sins of the world are too great. If only people knew what eternity is, they would do everything to change their lives. People lose their souls because they do not think about the death of Our Lord and do not do penance.

"Many marriages are not good; they do not please Our Lord and are not of God.

"Pray a great deal for governments. Pity those governments which persecute the religion of Our Lord. If governments left the Church in peace and gave liberty to the Holy Religion, they would be blessed by God.

"My good Mother, do not give yourself to immodest clothes. Run away from riches. Love holy poverty and silence very much. Be very charitable, even with those who are unkind. Never criticize others and avoid those who do. Be very patient, for patience brings us to Heaven. Mortifications and sacrifices please Our Lord a great deal.

"Confession is a sacrament of mercy. That is why people should approach the confessional with confidence and joy. Without confession, there is no salvation.

"The Mother of God wants a larger number of virgin souls to bind themselves to her by the vow of chastity. I would enter a convent with great joy but my joy is greater because I am going to Heaven. To be a religious, one has to be very pure in soul and in body."

"And do you know what it means to be pure?" the Superior asked.

"I do, yes, I do. To be pure in body means to preserve chastity. To be pure in soul means to avoid sin, not to look at what would be sinful, not to steal, never lie and always tell the truth even when it is hard. Whoever does not fulfill promises made to Our Lady will not be blessed in life."

The day had to come when Jacinta was taken from the care of Mother Godinho to go to the hospital. This parting meant a great deal to Jacinta, for she loved the Mother very much, but what hurt most was to have to leave Jesus. There was no chapel at the hospital, no one to whom she might go for consolation. Everyone proved to be very kind to her, but who could take the place of Mother Godinho or of Our Lord? Some days, she was very saddened by the worldliness of the visitors, the women dressed in fashionable clothes, often with low-

138

cut dresses. "What is it all for?" she asked Mother Godinho. "If they only knew what eternity is."

Some visitors were one day discussing in her presence the faults of a certain priest who had been forbidden to say Mass. Jacinta began to weep for sorrow and she said that people should not talk about priests but they should rather pray for them. She herself often prayed for priests and asked others to do the same.

Many doctors came to examine her, their only thought was of science and medicine. They discounted the influence God might have on the condition of a patient. The little girl did not hesitate to set them straight on the matter, pointing out the cause of their frequent failures. "Pity doctors. They have no idea what awaits them. Doctors do not know how to treat their patients with success because they have no love for God."

One day, a doctor requested her prayers for a special intention. "I will pray for you," she assured him, "but just remember that you are going to be taken away, and soon." She told another doctor the same thing about himself and his daughter.

One great joy awaited Jacinta in the hospital. Our Lady saw to it that her father might visit his child, if only for a few hours. He could not stay long because he had left the other children at home sick in bed. It broke his heart to see Jacinta alone in the hospital and to have to leave her, but he was fully convinced that Our Lady was caring for her.

When the doctors first mentioned an operation, Jacinta warned them that it would be useless.

"It is all in vain. Our Lady told me that I am going to die soon." She had even had someone write Lúcia informing her of the day and hour of her death. The doctors, however, insisted; and when she was finally taken to the operating room she was found too weak to take gas. Anaesthesia not being then what it is today, the local injection given her by no means took away her pain. Yet she appears to have suffered more from the humiliation of having to expose her body and to place herself into the hands of the strange doctors.

They removed two ribs and the doctors appeared hopeful of success, even though the open wound on her chest was the size of a fist. The wound had to be bathed and cleansed often and it was most painful. Jacinta allowed only one moan to escape her lips, "Oh, Our Lady! Oh! Our Lady! Patience. We must suffer to go to Heaven."

Though she suffered so much, she never complained, accepting it with happiness, for she realized it would help many souls to escape the terrible fire of Hell. "Now You can convert many sinners," she spoke to Our Lord, "for I suffer a great deal, my Jesus."

Our Lady continued to come to visit her often. Four days before her death, she said, "I am not complaining any more. Our Lady has appeared again and said that she was coming for me soon. She took all my pains away."

Doctor Lisboa testified to this. "Her pains disappeared completely. She felt inclined to play and busied herself with looking at a few religious pictures, among which was one of Our Lady of the Sameiro. She said it was the one which most resembled the Lady she had seen. It was given to me later as a souvenir of Jacinta. I was told a few times that the little child wanted to see me to reveal a secret. Busy as I was and hearing that

Jacinta was feeling better, I postponed my visit. Unhappily I did not see her."

Mother Godinho visited Jacinta every day, bringing with her different friends each time. If anyone happened to sit near the bed where Our Lady had stood, Jacinta would protest, "Please move aside for Our Lady stood there."

She was asked if she would not like to see her mother before she died. "My family will not live long and soon we will all meet in Heaven. Our Lady shall appear again but not to me, for I am going to die, of course, as Our Lady told me."

February the twentieth came. Jacinta seemed about the same; she might last a few more days, she might go any moment. About six o'clock in the evening the child said she was not feeling well and she wanted to receive the last rites of the Church. A priest was called, heard her confession and promised to bring her Communion in the morning. Jacinta asked him to bring it immediately but he could see no reason for alarm. She insisted that she was to die shortly. At ten-thirty, she died peacefully without having her wish fulfilled.

A young nurse by the name of Aurora Gomez was the only person with Jacinta at the time of her death. They loved each other dearly and Jacinta called her "Aurorinha." The nurse remained with the child's body all night and in the morning, dressed it in a white First Communion dress with a blue sash, as Jacinta had asked her to, for these were the colors of Our Lady. Doctor Lisboa thought that the Church might in due time officially accept the apparitions of Fátima and so he did not want her body laid away in a common grave. He went to the pastor of the local Church and after much persuasion prevailed upon him to allow the casket to be placed in one of the sacristies of the Church to await burial.

The news of the child's death spread fast through the city and crowds flocked to the Church to see the body. All wanted to touch Rosaries or statues to her body. The pastor would not allow this homage for he said that it belonged only to those saints canonized by the Church. He had the body removed to another room under lock and key. Crowds continued to come, however, and to placate them the undertaker took them into the room in small groups to view the body of the little girl who they were sure was already with Our Lord and Our Lady in Heaven.

The undertaker testified that he never before nor after had a case like Jacinta's. "It seems to me that I can still today see the little angel. Laid in the casket, she seemed to be still alive, in her full beauty with rosy cheeks and lips. I have seen many bodies in my business, young and old. Never did a thing of this sort happen to me before nor since. The pleasant aroma that exhaled from her body cannot be explained. The worst unbeliever could not question it. . . . Though the child had been dead three days, the aroma was like a bouquet of flowers."

Considering the serious nature of Jacinta's sickness and the poison that was in the system from the pleurisy, all of which would hasten corruption of the body, we can understand the undertaker's wonderment at this unusual phenomenon when Jacinta's body seemed exempted from this natural law. On the twenty-fourth, the body was placed in a leaden casket, sealed in the presence of the authorities and some ladies, and transferred to the family vault of a generous-hearted man from Ourem. Mother Godinho accompanied the body and thus was enabled to visit Fátima as Jacinta promised she would.

Ti Marto was at the station to meet the body. "When I saw so many people around the little casket of my Jacinta, it was all so nice, I burst into tears at the sight, just like a little child. I never cried so much in all my life. 'Nothing helped you,' I sobbed, 'nothing would cure you. You stayed here for two months, then you went to Lisbon . . . There you died alone, all alone . . .' "

Fifteen years later, on September 12, 1935, the Bishop of Leiria commanded that her body be transferred to the cemetery of Fátima where the bodies of Jacinta and Francisco were to be placed in the same tomb, built especially for the two children. When Jacinta's casket was opened on this occasion, her little body was still whole and incorrupt. She and Francisco had gone home to rest in the Hearts of Jesus and Mary to console them and to pray for the conversion of sinners, for the Holy Father, for priests, and for all who ask their prayerful assistance.

XIII. The Chapel at the Cova da Iria

AFTER OCTOBER 13, 1917, the Cova da Iria was never the same. Pilgrims were coming all the time. "They knelt before the holmoak," Maria da Capelinha re-

called, "they wept and prayed to Our Lady. When
there was a group, they sang hymns. They came to
ask favors of Our Lady and she heard them all.
No one was ever disappointed; no one felt tired. I
never heard in those days that Our Lady refused
anyone a grace. All those who came had faith. If
they did not have it, they caught it here. How
wonderful that time was. It brings tears to our eyes.
I remember once being approached by a man who
was soaking wet. I asked him if he was not feeling
well. He had spent the night in the open and the
day was cold and rainy. 'Not at all, lady,' he replied, 'I never had a night as happy as this one.
I have behind me twenty miles and I am not tired
at all. I feel very happy here at Fátima.' "

Almost from the beginning people had been leaving gifts of money and produce at the sacred spot
as tokens of their devotion and gratitude. On the
13th of August, on the occasion when the children
were absent, the crush of people around the little
tree was such that all these offerings were being
trammelled under foot, so Maria da Capelinha decided to save what she could, especially the money,
until some decision could be made as to its use.
She offered the money first to one of the elder
Marto boys, who flatly refused it. Then next day
she thought to give it to Senhor Marto. Arriving
at the Marto home, she found the Pastor there.
"I can still see him leaning against the wall," she
recalls. "I might have seemed a little discourteous,
but in my excitement, I went right to Ti Marto,
offering the money to him instead of to the Pastor.
Ti Marto, of course, refused. 'Don't try me any
more, lady,' he said. 'I have been tempted enough.' "
Senhor Olimpia also would have nothing to do with

144

it. Only then did Maria turn to the Pastor, and he also coldly turned it down.

"Well, it isn't mine," she insisted. "So I shall put it back just where I found it."

"Don't do that," advised the Pastor. "Keep it, or have someone else keep it until things clear up."

So Maria da Capelinha continued to collect the offerings each day, and to sell the produce, thus increasing the treasury. And as the funds increased the people spoke more and more of erecting a chapel at the Cova da Iria. As time passed, however, nothing was being done about the building. Of course, the civil authorities were absolutely opposed to the idea of a chapel, and the Church authorities were prudently indifferent. Meantime rumors began to go around to the effect that Maria da Capelinha was keeping the money for her family.

Maria then went to the Pastor to ask his advice. He showed her a letter from the Cardinal stating that the money be kept for the time being, but not by the parents, lest they be accused of profiting from the apparitions. Instead it should be kept by some other trustworthy person. The Pastor asked her to continue to retain the funds. Still the rumors continued and things came to a climax one day when Manuel Carreira, Maria's husband, was summoned to appear before the Magistrate. The poor man imagined all sorts of things, but nothing came of the interview except that it precipitated action on the part of those desirous of building a chapel. Senhor Santos readily donated the land, and within a month a pitifully small chapel was erected.

As soon as the chapel was finished, someone offered to have a statue made to complete the shrine. This proposal met with great enthusiasm, and immediately a procession was planned for the installation of the statue. It didn't take the hostile government officials long to learn of this, and forthwith they made their own plans for breaking up the demonstration. When the day of the procession arrived there was general commotion around the village church of Fátima, where the statue was to be brought. A sudden thunderstorm dispersed the government guards permitting the statue to be brought into the church, where it was blessed and venerated and then secreted for fear that it would be stolen. There was no procession. Meantime the niche in the chapel at the Cova was veiled to make it appear that the statue was already there. When nothing happened after a while, the statue was quietly moved to the niche.

Rumors started up again that everything would be stolen or set on fire, so Maria da Capelinha and her husband thought it best to take the statue to their home every night. Their fears were to be justified.

Two years later, on May 6, 1922, two bombs were placed at the Cova, one in the chapel, the other at the holmoak. The roof of the chapel was blown off, but the bomb at the holmoak failed to explode. According to Maria da Capelinha, the Bishop then forbade the rebuilding of the chapel. Consequently the people spent longer hours outside the Carreira home, where the statue was now kept.

"There was always someone there," says Senhora Capelinha, "and Our Lady continued to answer their petitions. This encouraged the people, and they wanted to have the statue returned to the Cova for the 13th of May." There being no litter on which it could be placed for the procession, everyone individually offered to carry it, to fulfill some promise or other to Our Lady. When the day of the 13th came, the procession was held, the people taking turns carrying the burden, while the crowd sang and prayed.

Meantime the destruction of the chapel had aroused the people to protest to the government, and they determined to hold a great pilgrimage for May 13th of the following year (1923) in order to make reparation to Our Lady for this terrible insult. Some officials tried to prevent the demonstration, but when the day arrived, over sixty thousand persons gathered to march to Fátima to pay homage to their Queen.

Thirty years have now passed since the apparitions occurred and the barren fields on which Lúcia, Francisco and Jacinta used to graze their sheep are now covered with large beautiful buildings. The little chapel can still be seen, but a great shrine in honor of Our Lady of Fátima in process of construction dominates the area, flanked by a hospital, a convent and a retreat house, all of which testify to the power and mercy of Our Blessed Mother Mary.

XIV. Lúcia's Mission

AFTER FRANCISCO AND JACINTA had gone home to Heaven, Lúcia felt all alone in the world. She remembered the consoling promise of Our Lady that she would never leave her alone but would be her constant comfort, but still her heart yearned for the pleasant companionship of her beloved cousins. Everything reminded her of them; the hills, the trees, the sheep, and especially the Cova da Iria. Besides, thousands upon thousands of visitors flocked to Fátima to visit the scene of the apparitions and all wanted to speak with Lúcia. They came to her home every hour of the day. They insisted upon learning every detail of the apparitions; how Our Lady looked, what she wore, what she said, everything. When Jacinta and Francisco were with her, it was easier to face all these people, but alone, oh, if only she could go away and be alone with Our Lord and Our Lady. And the one thing that hurt Lúcia perhaps more than everything else was that the constant stream of visitors disturbed and upset the peace of her home.

Meanwhile, in January, 1918, only three months after the last apparition, the Holy See, after a lapse of sixty years, reëstablished the Diocese of Leiria, Portugal, of which the village of Fátima is a part. The Reverend Joseph Correia da Silva was named Bishop and took possession of his See on August the fifth, 1920. Bishop Silva considered it his most important duty to obtain the complete facts on the Fátima apparitions so that he might safeguard and foster true devotion to God and His Mother. The Bishop moved slowly and prudently, refusing to make any decisions or to take any action except after long and prayerful deliberation. He investigated every source of information and had his first interview with Lúcia on the thirteenth of June, 1921.

Having heard about the frequent intrusions upon Lúcia and her family by the many visitors, he invited Lúcia and her mother to visit him. He then informed mother and daughter of his plan to send

148

Lúcia to a convent school where she would not be known and where no one would bother her. Besides, the Bishop considered that if the many cures and conversions that had already taken place at the Cova da Iria continued in Lúcia's absence, it would be an almost certain sign of Heaven's approbation. If not, the devotion would die of itself.

"You must not tell anyone when or where you are going," the Bishop said to Lúcia, informing her that she must leave within five days.

"Yes, Bishop," Lúcia respectfully replied.

"You must not tell a soul at school who you are."

"Yes, Bishop."

"And you must not utter a word about Fátima."

"Yes, Bishop." Lúcia would do whatever he commanded. And when she returned home with her mother, the few remaining days sped by ever so fast. She ardently wished to say good-bye to the Martos and to Senhora da Capelinha, but she had promised not to tell anyone of her going. She could, however, spend her time visiting the holy places where she and her cousins had spent so many happy days. The last day home, June the seventeenth, Lúcia went first to the rocks where the Angel had appeared. There she prostrated herself on the ground, repeating over and over again the simple prayer of the Angel, "My God, I believe, adore, hope and love You. I ask forgiveness for those who do not believe, do not adore, do not hope, and do not love You."

Lúcia then went to the Valinhos, where Our Lady appeared after the children's imprisonment. She knelt beside the little holmoak whereon Our Lady had stood, though the tree had long since been stripped of all its branches by pious pilgrims. She spent quite a while there, then arose from her knees, walked on past the bog and the little pond where the three used to graze their sheep, directing her steps towards the Cova da Iria. No one was there. How happy Lúcia was to be alone, to live again the enchantment of the heavenly apparitions. She again heard in her heart those beautiful, comforting words of Our Lady, "Don't be afraid, I shall not leave you. I will take you to Heaven . . . but you are to remain a longer time on earth, for Jesus wants to use you to make me known and loved. My Immaculate Heart will be your refuge and the way that will lead you to God."

Lúcia remained at the Cova so long, she did not realize the passing of time, the sun was setting on the far hills. She hastened to the little Chapel to make one last visit, then on to the Parish Church where she had been baptized and where she had so often attended Holy Mass and received Our Lord in Holy Communion. She knelt at the altar rail, thanking Our Lord for these wonderful privileges of her faith, then walked around the Church, stopping for a moment before each statue to bid good-bye to the many saints and to ask their help on her journey. Leaving the church, she journeyed to the grave of her beloved father, who had died some time past, then on to the grave of Francisco. How she loved her little cousin, Francisco. He was such a quiet boy, strong, manly, truthful and reliable, so much like St. Joseph must have been when he was a boy. She remembered his words to her before he died, "Lúcia, I am going to Heaven. Jacinta is going to pray a great deal for sinners, for the Holy Father and for you. You are going to stay here below because Our Lady wants you to. Do whatever she says." Lúcia promised she would.

The little girl then went home, had her supper and her mother sent her off to bed early. But Lúcia was too weary to sleep. Although she was eager to go away to pray and be alone with Jesus and Mary, it was not easy to leave her dear mother. She offered this sacrifice to save souls from Hell. At two o'clock in the morning her mother aroused her, helped her get ready and together they started on the long journey. The light of the moon and the beautiful stars lighted their way and as they neared the Cova da Iria, Lúcia said, "Mother, let's stop for a while and say our Rosary."

"All right, Lúcia," Senhora Santos answered, and together they went to recite their beads. When they finished, they resumed their journey to the city of Leiria where Lúcia was to take the train for Oporto. Her mother would leave her at the station, for the Bishop had appointed another woman to accompany Lúcia on the train and take her to the school. The scene at the station as mother and daughter said good-bye to each other was sad to watch for tears poured forth from their eyes, tears of deepest love and bitter sorrow. They knew not when they would again meet.

When Lúcia reached the convent school, the Mother Superior, under orders from the Bishop, gave Lúcia a new name. She was henceforth to be known as Maria das Dores, and no one would recognize her under that name. The Superior also warned her of the Bishop's injunctions never to tell who she was and not to speak of Fátima. Lúcia would gladly offer this sacrifice to Our Lady.

The girls at the school quickly grew to love Lúcia. They were drawn to her as the many children of

Fátima used to gather around her at home. And
though she never spoke of Fátima, she did speak
to them often of Our Lady, how beautiful and kind
she was and what all should do to please her. She
inspired in all an ardent love for Mary. And when
she finished her course of studies, she asked if she
might be admitted into the Order of the good sisters
who had taken care of her, the Sisters of St.
Dorothy. They were happy to welcome this sweet
and holy girl into their midst.

In the convent, Our Lady did not leave Lúcia
alone. She came to visit her many times. At the
Cova da Iria, Our Lady had already told Lúcia of
the bitter sorrow of her heart over the ingratitude
and sinfulness of mankind. She asked that the first
Saturday of each month be set aside by all as a day
of reparation to her Immaculate Heart. Our Lady
again appeared to Lúcia on December 10, 1925, while
she was in her room at the convent. The Child Jesus
was at Our Lady's side, elevated upon a cloud of
light. Our Lady, resting one hand upon Lúcia's shoulder, held in her other hand a heart surrounded with
sharp thorns. The Child Jesus spoke first to Lúcia:

*"Have pity on the Heart of your Most Holy
Mother. It is covered with the thorns with which
ungrateful men pierce it at every moment, and there
is no one to remove them with an act of reparation."*

Then Our Lady said to Lúcia: *"My Daughter,
look at my Heart encircled with the thorns with
which ungrateful men pierce it at every moment by
their blasphemies and ingratitude. Do you at least
try to console me and announce in my name that
I promise to assist at the hour of death with the
graces necessary for salvation all those who, on the*

152

first Saturday of five consecutive months, go to Confession and receive Holy Communion, recite the Rosary and keep me company for a quarter of an hour while meditating on the mysteries of the Rosary with the intention of making reparation to me."

Lúcia could never forget this vision of Mary's bleeding heart. She informed her confessor and her superior of this apparition but they felt unable of themselves to spread this devotion. A year passed, and on the fifteenth of December, 1926, the Child Jesus again appeared to Lúcia, inquiring if she had spread this devotion of reparation to the Immaculate Heart of His Mother. She told Our Lord how her confessor had pointed out to her so many difficulties, and though the Mother Superior ardently desired to propagate the devotion, her confessor also warned her that she could do nothing by herself.

"It is true that your superior alone can do nothing, but with My grace she can do all," Our Lord answered.

Lúcia meanwhile did her part to make this devotion known by writing her own mother, urging her to become an apostle in the crusade of reparation:

"Dear Mother," her letter began, "as I know my letters always bring you great consolation, I am writing to you now to urge you to offer Our Lord the sacrifice of my absence. I know truly how deeply you feel this separation. However, you must realize that, if we did not separate from each other willingly, Our Lord would have taken it upon Himself to do it. Let us remember Uncle Manuel, who said that he would never allow his children to leave home, and Our Lord took them away.

"This is why I wanted you, Mother, to offer our

153

separation to Our Lady generously, as an act of
reparation for the offenses she receives from her ungrateful children. I desired that you, Mother, might
give me the consolation of embracing the devotion
which I know pleases God and which Our Lady herself requested.

"As soon as I knew it, I embraced it myself and
have wanted to do everything possible to make
others practice it. I expect that you will write to me
saying that you have accepted it and are trying to
make others take up this devotion. You can never
give me a greater consolation. It consists only in
what is written on the back of the enclosed little
stamp. Confession can be made on another day. The
fifteen minutes of meditation are what will puzzle
you most, but it is very easy. Who is the person who
cannot think upon the mysteries of the Rosary? The
Annunciation of the Angel and the humility of our
dear Mother, who, when she was exalted, called
herself the handmaiden of the Lord? Who cannot
meditate on the sufferings of Our Lord, Who suffered
so much in His love for us and Our Lady near Jesus
on Calvary? Who is the one who cannot spend fifteen minutes near the most tender of mothers, reflecting on these thoughts?

"Good-bye, dearest Mother. Console our dear
heavenly Mother in this manner and do your best
to get others to console her. In this way you will
give me unbounded joy. Your most devoted child,
who kisses your hand. Lúcia de Jesús."

When she spoke of this devotion to one priest, he
remarked that Our Lady used more or less the same
words that Our Lord used when He made His promises to St. Margaret Mary with regard to the Nine
First Fridays. Lúcia merely smiled, saying, "Can I

tell the Blessed Virgin how she is to express herself?"

Lúcia had not yet been given permission to reveal all that Our Lady had spoken to her at the Cova da Iria. She did, however, have permission to reveal the need of reparation and the devotion of the First Saturdays. It was in 1927, while she was praying in the convent chapel at Tuy, Spain, where she was then stationed, that she received permission from Heaven to reveal the first two parts of the secret, the vision of Hell and the urgent need for devotion to the Immaculate Heart of Mary. "You have seen Hell where the souls of poor sinners go. To save them, God wants to establish throughout the world the devotion to my Immaculate Heart. . . . I shall come to ask the consecration of Russia to my Immaculate Heart."

Lúcia informed her confessors, her Mother Provincial, the Bishop of Leiria and the Reverend Joseph Galamba of this. The third part of the secret revealed to the three children at the Cova da Iria on July 13, 1917, has not yet been revealed. According to instructions from above, Lúcia has written it down. It was sealed and by order of the Bishop of Leiria placed in his diocesan archives. No one but Lúcia knows its contents and it is to be opened and read in 1960.

Two years later, in 1929, Our Lady again appeared to Lúcia while she was praying in the chapel at Tuy. This was the time chosen by Our Lady to ask the fulfillment of her previous request: "I shall come to ask the consecration of Russia to my Immaculate Heart. . . . If they heed my request, Russia will be converted and there will be peace." Our Lady explained that this consecration should be made by the Holy Father in unison with all the bishops of the world.

Lúcia made known this request to her confessors. One of them, the Reverend Francisco Rodrigues, S.J., told her to write it down. He showed this letter to the Bishop and gave him the full details. Father Rodrigues also had it brought to the attention of the Holy Father.

Three years passed during which nothing was accomplished. Lúcia again wrote to the Bishop, adding the words of Our Lord, "As long as the King of France did not listen to my request (when He asked St. Margaret Mary to obtain the consecration of France to the Sacred Heart by the king) the Holy Father will consecrate Russia to Me, but it will be late."

Ten years passed. Pope Pius XI died in the spring of 1939 and the war began in September of that same year. Lúcia had warned that war was to begin under the reign of Pius XI. Father Jongen asked her if Our Lady really mentioned the Pope's name. "Yes, Our Lady pronounced his name," said Lúcia. "We did not know whether it meant a Pope or a king. However, Our Lady did speak of Pius XI."

"But the war did not begin under Pius XI," Father Jongen countered.

"The annexation of Austria gave occasion for the war," replied Lúcia. "When the Munich Accord was made, the sisters rejoiced for they thought that peace was secured. Unhappily, I knew more than they."

"And what about that great sign that God was going to give the world that He was going to punish it for its crimes?"

156

Lúcia answered that this sign was the appearance of the "Great Northern Lights" of 1938 when unusual lights appeared in the skies of the world. "This was the sign," she said, "that God used to make me understand that His justice was ready to deal the blow upon the guilty nations."

"But the astronomers say that it was a common aurora borealis," the priest countered.

"I do not know, but it seems to me that if they had studied it well, they would have realized that, owing to the circumstances under which the light appeared, it was not nor could it have been an aurora borealis." Meanwhile World War II was raging throughout Europe, threatening to engulf the whole world.

In 1940, Lúcia wrote again to the Bishop of Leiria expressing her regret that the consecration had not yet been made. "Would that the world knew the hour of grace that is being given it and would do penance." Then she wrote directly to Pope Pius XII at the command of her spiritual directors, telling him the exact request of Our Lady. Lúcia asked for the consecration of the world to Mary's Immaculate Heart with a special mention of Russia. The Pope deliberated long and prayerfully upon this request of Mary. In 1942, the clergy and people of Portugal celebrated the silver anniversary of the apparitions of Fátima. On the last day of October of the same year, the Bishops gathered at the Cathedral of Lisbon to join with the Holy Father in fulfilling the request of Our Lady. The Pope at that time consecrated the Church and the world to her Immaculate Heart, including the people of Russia by these words: "Give peace to the peoples separated from us by error or by schism and especially to the one who professes such singular devotion to thee and in whose homes an honored place was ever accorded thy venerable icon (today perhaps often kept hidden to await better days); bring them back to the one fold of Christ under the one true Shepherd. . . ." Six weeks later, on the Feast of the Immaculate Conception, in the presence of 40,000 people, the Holy Father repeated this consecration at St. Peter's in Rome. This consecration was a decisive event in the history of the world; it marks the beginning of a new era, the Age of Mary.

The following spring, Our Blessed Lord appeared to Lúcia to express the joy of His Heart over this consecration. Lúcia tells about it in her letter to the Bishop of Gurza, her spiritual director. Therein we begin to realize how this consecration marked the change in the course of history. World War II that threatened to go on interminably, with its wholesale and inhuman destruction, was to end soon. And at the moment of greatest danger, when the extinction of all people by atomic bombs was at hand, the war stopped abruptly on the Feast of Our Lady!

"Your Excellency," Lúcia wrote, "The good Lord has already shown me His pleasure in the act of the Holy Father and the various Bishops, although incomplete according to His desire. In exchange, He promises to bring the war soon to an end, but the conversion of Russia will not take place yet: if the Bishops of Spain heed the desires of Our Lord and engage in a true reform of the people . . . good; if not, she (Russia) will again be the enemy with which God shall punish them once more.

"The good Lord is allowing himself to be appeased, but He complains bitterly and sorrowfully about the small number of souls in His grace who are willing to renounce whatever the observance of His Law requires of them.

"This is the penance which the good Lord now asks: the sacrifice that every person has to impose upon himself is to lead a life of justice in the observance of His Law. He requires that this way be made known to souls. For many, thinking that the word penance means great austerities and not feeling in themselves the strength or generosity for these, lose heart and rest in a life of lukewarmness and sin.

"Last Thursday, at midnight, while I was in chapel with my superiors' permission, Our Lord said to me, *'The sacrifice required of every person is the fulfillment of his duties in life and the observance of My law. This is the penance that I now seek and require.'*"

Our Lord said the act of the Holy Father is incomplete but it cannot be completed until every individual, every home, every diocese and every country consecrates itself, after the example of the Holy Father, to the Immaculate Heart. For as the Bishop of Leiria wrote, "At the request of the Bishops of Portugal and of Sister Lúcia herself, the Holy Father, in the course of his famous message to Portugal at the close of the Fátima Jubilee on October 31, 1942, made the consecration of the world to the Immaculate Heart of Mary, a consecration which we all must repeat officially and personally."

This personal consecration has four essential elements, grace, penance, the Rosary and reparation. "Our Lord complained bitterly and sorrowfully about the small number of souls in His grace. . . ." Our Lady came to bring peace to the world and

159

the foundation of peace is the possession of grace. Wars are only punishment for the sins of the world. Grace makes man holy and pleasing to God. Only when grace illumines man's soul is there peace between God and man. And when peace reigns between God and man, Mary will reward the world with peace.

To persevere in this peace and the grace of God, man need not perform heroic sacrifices as did the children of Fátima; rather, they must fulfill their daily duties in life. And because these duties are oftentimes hard and burdensome, they become works of penance and sacrifice. "The sacrifice required of every person is the fulfillment of his duties in life and the observance of My law. This is that penance that I now seek and require." In the Gospel, Our Lord speaks of this as man's "daily cross." "If any man will come after Me, let him deny himself, and take up his cross daily, and follow Me." (Luke 9:23)

An essential element in the life of Christ was a deep love of His Mother, Mary. So the true disciple of Christ must share in this love for Mary and prove it in his daily life through the recitation of the Rosary. The person who says his beads sincerely is bound to be pleasing to God and draws God's grace unto himself. Also, the Rosary gives Mary new power to crush the head of the Serpent and to destroy his evil power over the world.

Communions of Reparation are also required for the fulfillment of this personal consecration to Our Lady. It was no mere coincidence that Our Lord requested the Communions of Reparation on the First Saturdays in almost the same words that He used when He spoke to St. Margaret Mary about the First Fridays. He desires that this devotion to the Immaculate Heart of Mary be made known and spread throughout the world and that it become a common practice like that of the First Fridays. Men must all gather around Mary, as if on Calvary with John and Mary Magdalene, to console her Heart, and by the offering of their Rosary, their daily sacrifices and the practice of the First Saturdays, remove the thorns with which ungrateful men pierce her Immaculate Heart at every moment.

When these requirements for the personal consecration are lived by each person, then the consecration made by the Holy Father will be realized. Then we will become, as Our Lady desires, true crusaders in the cause of justice and truth. Then we will be cooperating with her in the redemption of the world and in the work of peace.

Appendix I

Father Formigão's First Interview

MONSIGNOR QUARESMA and Father Gois were not the only priests sincerely interested in studying the visions of the children. The Reverend Manuel Nunes Formigão, a Canon of the Lisbon Cathedral and a professor of the Seminary, had been commissioned by the Archbishop of Mytilene, D. João de Lima Vidal, the Governor of the Patriarchate during the exile of the Cardinal Patriarch, to investigate the unusual occurrences at Fátima. He witnessed the happenings at the Cova da Iria on September the thirteenth from the road, about 200 yards distant from the holmoak, and noticed only the dimming of the sun, which he attributed to the altitude of the hills. Unwilling to form a judgment on his own, he decided to gather information from other witnesses, and determined to get the whole story from the children. Two weeks later, on the 27th of September, he interviewed the children. Kind and courteous, he won their confidence. Francisco was the first to be questioned.

"Tell me, Francisco, what did you see at the Cova da Iria these last few months?"

"I saw Our Lady."

"Where does she appear?"

"Over a holmoak."

"Does she appear suddenly or do you see her come from some place?"

"I see her come from the side where the sun rises and she stands over the holmoak." The eight-year-old boy did not know the full meaning of the words east and west. He used his own simple language.

"Does she come slowly or fast?"

"She always comes fast."

"Do you hear what she says to Lúcia?"

"I do not hear."

"Did you ever speak with the Lady? Has she spoken to you?"

"No, I never asked anything. She speaks only to

Lúcia." [8] Francisco was a quiet, thoughtful boy. The inference is that, if he wished, he could have spoken to her and she would have spoken to him. He was satisfied to be silent, but heart speaks to heart when the tongue is silent.

"Whom does she look at?" the priest went on, "at you also, and Jacinta, or at Lúcia only?"

"She looks at the three of us, but she looks longer at Lúcia."

"How is she dressed?"

"She has a long dress and a mantle over it which covers her head and runs down to the edge of the dress."

"What is the color of the dress and mantle?"

"It is white and the dress has golden stripes."

"What is the attitude of the Lady?"

"It is of one who is praying. She has her hands joined before her breast."

"Does she hold anything in her hands?"

"She holds beads between the palm and the back of her right hand which hang down over her dress."

"Has she anything on her ears?"

"The ears are not seen because they are covered by the mantle."

"What color are the beads?"

"They are white too."

[8] Maria da Capelinha one day asked Lúcia a question that to her had long been a riddle. "Lúcia, why does Our Lady speak only with you and not with Jacinta and Francisco?"

"But Jacinta is very retiring and does not speak. If she spoke, Our Lady would speak with her also."

Jacinta looked at Senhora Carreira and at Lúcia. She did not say a word but smiled.

It seems, however, that there is a deep motive in the fact that Our Lady speaks with Lúcia who hears and sees, in the fact that Jacinta sees and hears but does not speak and in the fact that Francisco sees Our Lady but does not speak or hear her.

Lúcia is the leader; to her is entrusted a most important mission. She is to remain a longer time in the world to make the Immaculate Heart of Mary known and loved throughout the world. Jacinta and Francisco depend upon Lúcia. They are a part of Lúcia's mission. Also, Lúcia was in the light of Mary spreading over the world, Francisco and Jacinta in the light ascending to Heaven. So Lúcia is for the world, while the other two are for Heaven, to console God and Our Lady.

There is another providential reason in this distinction of role. It stops the argument of those who claimed there was collusion or collective hallucinations on the part of the children.

163

"Has she ever wept or smiled?"

"Neither one thing or the other. She is always serious."

"Is the Lady beautiful?"

"She is."

"Is she more beautiful than that girl that you see over there?" the priest said, pointing to a girl nearby.

"More," Francisco answered, his simplicity vouching for his truthfulness.

"But there are women more beautiful than that girl," the priest continued.

"Our Lady is more beautiful than anyone I ever saw." In saying this, Francisco felt he had said everything. What more could he say than that Our Lady is beyond all human comparisons. Her beauty and loveliness surpass earthly descriptions.

The priest then called Jacinta who was outside playing with the other children. She came in, sat on a stool next to Father Formigão and was glad to answer his questions.

"Have you seen Our Lady on the thirteenth day of each month since May?"

"I have, Father."

"Where does she come from?"

"From Heaven, from the side of the sun," the seven-year-old child answered.

"How is she dressed?"

"She has a white dress, enriched with gold and a mantle over her head which is also white."

"What is the color of her hair?"

"Her hair is not seen. It is covered with the mantle."

"Does she wear earrings?"

"I do not know because her ears are not seen."

"What is the position of her hands?"

"Her hands are joined at the breast with the fingers turned upwards."

"Has she the beads on the right or the left hand?"

Jacinta said Our Lady held them in her right hand but when the priest kept questioning her on this point, she became all confused and would not say which of her hands corresponded with the hand holding the beads in the apparition. The priest continued.

"What did Our Lady recommend to Lúcia above all?"

164

"She told us to say the Rosary every day."

"And do you say it?"

"I say it every day with Francisco and Lúcia." The priest was satisfied with Jacinta's answers, but she was so timid and shy, he did not wish to inquire any further. There was quite a contrast between Jacinta and Lúcia, who came in a little later. She was tall, strong and healthy, better developed than her cousins with a lighter complexion. Though she was tired looking and worn out from the unending stream of visitors and their repeated questions, she came into the room without any show of vanity or embarrassment. The priest requested her to sit down and she was patient and gracious to answer every question.

"Is it true that Our Lady appeared to you at the place called the Cova da Iria?"

"It is true."

"How often has she appeared to you?"

"Five times, once a month."

"Was it always on the thirteenth?"

"Always on the thirteenth, except August, when I was arrested and taken to the County House by the magistrate. That month I saw her only a few days after at Valinhos."

"It is said that Our Lady appeared to you last year also. Is this true?"

"She did not appear to me last year, neither before May of this year. I did not tell that to anyone for it is not true." The children hated lies with all their heart.

"Where does the Lady come from? From the east?"

"I do not know," Lúcia responded directly. "I do not see her come from anywhere. She appears over the holmoak; and when she leaves, it is then that she takes the direction of the side of Heaven where the sun rises."

"Does she stay for a long or short time?"

"A short time."

"Enough to say one *Our Father* and one *Hail Mary* or more?"

"More, much more; but not always the same space of time. Maybe it would not have been enough to say the Rosary." Lúcia wanted to be exact in every detail.

"Were you frightened the first time you saw Our Lady?"

"I was. I was so scared that I wanted to run away with Jacinta and Francisco. But she told us not to be afraid as she would not do us any harm."

"How was she dressed?"

"She has a white dress which comes down almost to her feet and her head is covered with a mantle of the same color and size as the dress."

"Isn't her dress adorned?"

"In front, there are seen two gilt strings running down from around her neck which join in a tassel, also made of gold, half way down."

"Has the dress any sash?"

"It has not."

"Does she wear earrings?"

"She has small earrings." Lúcia alone saw the earrings because she was directly facing Our Lady while the other children were looking at her more from an angle and could not see her ears under the mantle.

"Which of the hands holds the beads?"

"The right hand."

"Was it a full Rosary, fifteen decades, or just five?"

"I did not look closely.

"Did the beads end in a cross?"

"They ended in a white cross and the chain and the beads also were white."

"Did you ever ask her who she was?"

"I did ask her, but she told me that she would only tell it on the thirteenth of October."

"Did you not ask her where she came from?"

"I asked her where she was from and she answered from Heaven."

"When did you ask her that?"

"The second time, the thirteenth of June."

"Did she ever smile or become sad?"

"She never smiled nor showed herself sad. She was always serious."

"Did Our Lady recommend any prayers to you or your cousins?"

"She recommended that we say the Rosary in honor of Our Lady of the Rosary, to earn peace for the world."

"And did she wish that many people go to the Cova da Iria every month to be present at the apparitions?"

166

"She said nothing about that."

"Is it true that she has revealed a secret to you and has forbidden you to tell it to anyone?"

"That is true."

"Does the secret regard you only or your cousins also?"

"The three of us."

"Can you not reveal the secret at least to your confessor?" Lúcia was silent, she looked puzzled. Father Formigão did not think it right to insist. He continued.

"It is said that the day you were arrested, to get away from the magistrate, you told him something making believe it was the secret and it was not; that you deceived him and boasted of your trick afterwards. Is this true?"

"It is not." Lúcia vehemently denied such calumny. "In fact," Lúcia went on, "the magistrate wanted me to tell him the secret. Even though he insisted with me, I did tell him all that Our Lady had told me, except the secret. I did not want to deceive him." Again we see the child's intense love for the truth.

"Did the Lady tell you to learn to read?"

"Yes, the second time that she appeared."

"But if she told you that she would take you to Heaven in October, what is the use of learning to read?"

"That is not true. The Lady never told me that she would take me to Heaven in October; and I never said that she told me such a thing."

"What did the Lady say should be done with the money that the people leave near the holmoak at the Cova da Iria?"

"She said that we should put it on two litters. Jacinta and I and two girls would carry one of them, Francisco with three boys the other. Part of that money should be set aside for the feast of Our Lady of the Rosary and the other part should be set aside to help build the new chapel."

"Where does the Lady want the chapel built? At the Cova da Iria?"

"I do not know. She did not say."

"Are you not very happy because Our Lady has appeared to you?"

"I am."

"Will only Our Lady come on the thirteenth of
October?"

"Saint Joseph will come also with the Baby, and a
little afterwards peace shall be given to the world."

"Has Our Lady made any other revelations?"

"She declared that on October the thirteenth, she will
perform a miracle so that the people will believe that
she appears."

"Tell me, why do you lower your eyes so often during
the apparitions? Why do you take your eyes from the
Lady?"

"Because sometimes she blinds."

"Has she taught you any prayers?"

"Yes, and she wants us to say it after each decade of
the Rosary."

"Do you know it by heart?"

"Yes."

"Tell me what it is."

"O My Jesus, forgive us; save us from the fire of
Hell. Bring all souls to Heaven, especially those in most
need."

Appendix II

Father Jongen's Interview *

1. Concerning the Angel

"Are you absolutely sure that the Angel appeared to
you?"

"I saw him," Lúcia responded.

"The total silence of you three children concerning
these apparitions prevents many from giving them cre-
dence."

"It is not true that we never spoke to anyone about
them."

"To whom then did you reveal the apparitions?"

"First to the Dean of Olival. I trusted him and did

* This interview was conducted in January, 1946.

not hide anything from him. He advised me to keep them secret."

"Did you follow his advice?"

"Yes, and we revealed them only to the Bishop of Leiria."

"What did he say?"

"He, too, advised secrecy."

"Why did you not speak to anyone about the Angel at the time of the apparitions?"

"I and the other girls saw the Angel vaguely in 1915. Francisco and Jacinta were not with us. I did not speak of this apparition to anyone but the other girls did and people mocked us. It was a lesson which I had not forgotten when the Angel appeared to us in 1916. We decided to keep it secret."

"That is natural, but the priest who interviewed you recently on the matter finds it hard to explain the fact that three children so young could have kept a secret for so long."

"He would not if he had gone through all we did."

"What do you mean?"

"After hearing through Jacinta of Our Lady's first apparition, many plagued us unceasingly with detailed and captious questions. As they ridiculed everything, we decided to say only that we had seen Our Lady. If they asked us what Our Lady said, we would answer that she desired that everyone say the Rosary and we added nothing else."

"That was a good reason for not divulging the apparitions but only for a while. Why were they not made known before 1936?"

"The Dean of Olival, the Bishop of Leiria, circumstances, everything urged us to be silent. Shouldn't I wait until the Bishop made me speak?"

2. Concerning the Secret

"When did you receive permission from Heaven, as you say in your Memoirs, to reveal the secret?"

"It was in 1927, here in Tuy (Spain), while in the Chapel."

"Did you tell your confessor about it?"

"Immediately."

"What did he say?"

"He told me to write the secret with the exception of the third part. I think he did not read it; he returned it to me. A little later, I had another confessor who ordered me to burn it. Then he told me to write it again."

"It is regretful that the secret was not published before the war, for then Our Lady's prediction would have had more value.[9] Why did you not make it known before?"

"No one asked me for the secret."

"To whom else did you reveal the secret before the war?"

"To Mother Provincial, the Bishop of Leiria and the Reverend Joseph Galamba."

"Did you reveal everything without exception?"

"I cannot remember."

"Did you give only the general sense of what Our Lady told you or did you quote her words literally?"

"When I speak of the apparitions, I limit myself only to the general sense of the words. When I write, on the contrary, I take care to quote literally. And so I wanted to write the secret word by word."

"Are you sure you kept everything in your memory?"

"I think so."

"Were the words of the secret revealed in the same order they were communicated to you?"

"Yes."

3. Concerning the Consecration

"According to the text of the secret, Our Lady said, 'I shall come to ask the consecration of Russia to my Immaculate Heart and the Communion of Reparation on the First Saturdays.' Has she truly come to ask for the consecration?"

[9] Some will say, "Too late, too late, these warnings of Fátima should have been broadcast throughout the world years ago, and so the terrible destruction of World War II would have been prevented." But the world has had the Gospel of Peace preached to it for twenty centuries and yet little has been done by men to accomplish its ideals. Our Lord did not give Lúcia to the world as a prophetess, but as a messenger calling the world to penance and reparation.

"Yes."

"Did Our Lady in her apparition of 1925 speak of the consecration of Russia to her Immaculate Heart?"

"No."

"Then, when did that apparition take place?"

"In 1929."

"Where did it happen?"

"At Tuy, while in the chapel."

"What did Our Lady ask?"

"The consecration of Russia to the Immaculate Heart of Mary by the Pope, in union with all the Bishops of the world."

"Did she ask for the consecration of the world?"

"No."

"Did you inform the Bishop of Leiria about Our Lady's desires?"

"Yes, in 1929, I transmitted Our Lady's desire to my confessors, the Reverend Joseph G. Goncalves and the Reverend Francisco Rodrigues. Father Rodrigues told me to write it, gave a full account of it to the Bishop of Leiria, and had it brought to the attention of the Holy Father, Pius XI. In the letter which I wrote by order of my spiritual directors to the Holy Father in 1940 (Pius XII), I exposed the exact request of Our Lady and asked the consecration of the world with a special mention of Russia. The exact request of Our Lady was that the Holy Father consecrate Russia to her Immaculate Heart, ordering that this be made at the same time and in union with him by all the Bishops of the Catholic world."

In April 1947, in answer to the question whether the consecration of Russia by the Holy Father had been made in accordance with the conditions set by Our Lady for the conversion of Russia, Lúcia wrote: "Regarding the question relative to Russia, the Holy Father knows Our Lady's desire, and it is up to His Holiness that belongs any decision about what must be done."

171

Appendix III

Filomena Miranda's Interview *

1. Did Our Lady appear over the holmoak at the same time that you saw the flash?
   At the same time.
2. Did the flash last as long as the apparition?
   No.
3. Did the atmosphere have the same degree of light it had before the apparition? Were there any storm clouds (thunder)?
   No, it was not an atmosphere of thunder. Only claps of thunder were heard and the flash was seen afterwards.
4. Was the sky blue?
   It was clear.
5. Did Our Lady have any globe or cloud under her feet?
   No, Our Lady appeared enveloped in a light over the holmoak. The holmoak was about this high (showing the height with her hand).
6. How was Our Lady dressed?
   White all over.
7. White as snow?
   Her dress was brilliant.
8. Did it reach to her feet?
   Not quite. It was this way (Lucia showed the lady).
9. Did it reach up to her neck?
   Yes.
10. Did Our Lady's dress have any embroidery of gold or stars?
    It had an edge of gold around it, this way. . . . (She explained, about a third of an inch wide.) And there were stars (indicating how they were spaced), one almost at her waist, another half way down, another over her feet near the border of her dress.
11. Were the stars brilliant?
    Yes.

* Interview given by Lúcia in 1921 to Senhora Filomena Miranda who desired to make a painting of our Lady of Fátima.

172

12. Were they large?
No, they were small as this (explaining with her fingers).
13. Were they about the size of my watch?
Yes.
14. Did the stars have five rays of sparkling light or more?
(Lúcia thought for a while, then said) I did not look close.
15. Did Our Lady wear a sash?
She had a gold cord that ran down from her neck this way (explaining with a gesture of her hands). It ended in a gold tassel, about her waist.
16. The sleeves were somewhat wide?
They were this way (explaining).
17. Did Our Lady have a cloak?
She had a white cloak, of light.
18. Did the cloak trail over any cloud?
No.
19. Did it have any stars or gold embroidery?
It had only an edge of gold all around it, this size (about a third of an inch).
20. Did the cloak fall straight?
Yes, it was the same size as her dress.
21. How did Our Lady's hair look?
It was not seen. The cloak covered her head this way (explaining).
22. Had Our Lady ear-rings with bright jewels?
(Lucia thought for a while and said) I am not sure.
23. Had Our Lady the Rosary on her hand or on her arm?
Our Lady had her hands joined this way (explaining, pressed together before her breast, turned upwards). The Rosary hung down from her hand.
24. In which of her hands?
The right one.
25. Was the Rosary of gold?
It was white and shone with a white crucifix.
26. And was the crucifix sparkling?
Yes.
27. Was the Rosary large?
About like this. It reached almost to the second star on her dress.

173

28. Were the beads round or did they look like stars?
   They were round.
29. Were they all alike?
   The Paters *were a little larger.*
30. Was the chain of the Rosary sparkling also?
   Yes.
31. Did the beads shine with a light equal to that of
   the stars?
   They sparkled.
32. Was the crucifix as brilliant as the beads?
   Yes.
33. Did the Rosary have any star before the last three
   Hail Marys?
   Yes and it shone as a star.
34. Was there any star above the crucifix?
   No, just a bead at a little distance.
35. Was the head of Our Lady surrounded by an edge
   of gold with brilliant stars?
   Our Lady was enveloped in light.
36. Was it an incomparable light?
   Yes, Our Lady was brilliant all over.
37. Was the face of Our Lady white as the snow?
   It was brilliant (sparkling).
38. Are there words to explain it?
   No.
39. The eyes of Our Lady, were they blue or brown?
   I did not look closely.

The artist, Filomena, then told Lúcia she did not know
how she could paint a picture of Our Lady as she was
described by her. "Paint as you will," Lúcia responded,
meaning she should try to do the best possible.

40. Were her hands white?
   *They were brilliant and she had her hands joined
   this way . . .*
41. And the feet?
   Also brilliant.
42. Was there any flower or star about Our Lady's
   feet?
   *Her feet were enveloped in the same light which
   enveloped Our Lady.*
43. Were the dress and the cloak of silk?
   They were of light.

174

44. Did Our Lady look sad?
She had a serious expression.
45. Was she looking towards Heaven?
She looked at us.
46. Was the face of Our Lady very fine, very delicate?
Yes.
47. When Our Lady disappeared, was it suddenly?
She appeared suddenly but disappeared slowly.
48. Did any angel hold her cloak?
No.
49. Did Our Lady come on any cloud?
Our Lady was always enveloped in that light.
50. Was the light that enveloped Our Lady like brilliant clouds or was it a light like that of lightning? Did any rays of light like those of the brilliant rays of the sun issue forth from the light that enveloped Our Lady?
The light was a round light.
51. Was Our Lady's face as brilliant as the stars?
It was brilliant.
52. The statue that is at Fátima seems to have over her dress another dress with larger sleeves and has an embroidered cloak. Was it that way that you saw Our Lady?
No, Our Lady had only the dress and the cloak. They wanted the statue to be that way with that embroidery on the cloak.
53. The statue is over a cloud and I do not know what I shall put at Our Lady's feet.
Lúcia said that the best thing was to paint Our Lady over the holmoak as that was the way she appeared.
54. Did Our Lady appear close to you?
Yes.

Bibliography

AMEAL, JOÃO: *Historia de Portugal.* Porto, 1942
AZEVEDO, CARLOS: *Porque apareceu Nossa Senhora em Fátima.* Leiria, 1944
Broteria, XII, 1931, p. 79
COUTINHO, BERNARDO X.: *Album da Exposição de Arte Sacra.* Porto, 1944
DEL RIO, JOSÉ DE CASTRO (O.M.C.): *As Aparições da Santissima Virgem em Fátima.* Porto, 1946
DIAS, ANTONIO A. (S.J.): *Florilegio de Fátima.* Porto, 1945
EUDES, JOHN (SAINT): *Sacred Heart of Jesus,* Chapt. IV. New York, 1946
The Admirable Heart of Mary. New York, 1948
FAZENDA, ANTONIO A. (S.J.): *Meditações dos primeiros Sabados.* Braga, 1944
FELIX, JOSÉ M.: *Fátima e a Redenção de Portugal.* Famalicão, 1939
Santa Maria de Portugal. Lisboa, 1943
FIGUEIREDO, ANTERO DE: *Fátima.* Lisboa, 1943
FISCHER, LUIS: *Fátima, a Lourdes Portuguesa.* Lisboa, 1930
Fátima á luz da Autoridade Eclesiastica. Lisboa, 1932
FONSECA, LUIS G. A. (S.J.): *Nossa Senhora de Fátima.* Porto, 1934
FORMIGÃO, MANUEL N. [VISCONDE DE MONTELO] *A Perola de Portugal.* Lisboa, 1929
As grandes maravilhas de Fátima. Lisboa, 1927
Fátima, o Paraiso da Terra. Lisboa, 1930
Os acontecimentos de Fátima. Guarda, 1923
Os episodios maravilhosos de Fátima. Guarda, 1921
O que é Fátima. Braga, 1936
FORNASSARI, EUGENIO: *A grande Promessa.* Lisboa, 1946
MARCHI, JOÃO DE (I.M.C.): *Era uma Senhora mais brilhante que o sol.* Cova da Iria, 1947
OLIVEIRA, JOSÉ GALAMBA: *Fátima a prova.* Leiria, 1946
Jacinta. Leiria, 1946
PIZARRO, G. (S.J.): *Notre Dame de Fátima.* Louvain, 1930
ROLIM, JOSÉ (O.F.M.): *Francisco.* Lisboa, 1947

176

SHEEN, FULTON J.: *Calvary and the Mass,* Part IV. New
    York, 1936
SILVA, CLEMENTE P.: *O Imaculado Coracao e o Aposto-
    lado.* Braga, 1943
SILVIO, J.: *A mensagem da Virgem.* Braga, 1945
TAVARES, JOAQUIM DA S.: *Fátima e Lourdes.* Lisboa, 1931
    Voz de Fatima. Leiria, (n.d.)
ZUQUETE, AFONSO: *Leiria, subsidios para a historia da
    sua Diocese.* Leiria, 1946

SHEEN, FULTON J.: *Calvary and the Mass*, Part IV. New
York, 1936
SILVA, CLEMENTE P.: *O Imaculado Coracao e o Aposto-
lado*. Braga, 1943
SILVIO, J.: *A mensagem da Virgem*. Braga, 1945
TAVARES, JOAQUIM DA S.: *Fátima e Lourdes*. Lisboa, 1931
Voz de Fatima. Leiria, (n.d.)
ZUQUETE, AFONSO: *Leiria, subsidios para a historia da
sua Diocese*. Leiria, 1946

177

CPSIA information can be obtained
at www.ICGtesting.com
Printed in the USA
BVHW051457240720
584413BV00005B/263

9 781163 181966